ILLUSTRATOR CS2

ROBERT SHUFFLEBOTHAM

BARNES & NOBLE BOOKS

NEW YORK

In easy steps is an imprint of Computer Step
Southfield Road · Southam
Warwickshire CV47 0FB · United Kingdom
www.ineasysteps.com

This edition published for Barnes & Noble Books, New York
FOR SALE IN THE USA ONLY
www.bn.com

Notice of Liability
Every effort has been made to ensure that this book contains accurate and current information. However, Computer Step and the author shall not be liable for any loss or damage suffered by readers as a result of any information contained herein.

Trademarks
Adobe® and Illustrator® are registered trademarks of Adobe Systems Incorporated. All other trademarks are acknowledged as belonging to their respective companies.

Printed and bound in the United Kingdom

ISBN 0-7607-7858-2

Table of Contents

Arranging Objects 61

Color and Appearance Attributes 79

Cutting and Joining Paths 95

The Working Environment

Adobe Illustrator is a powerful drawing application which you can use to produce anything from the simplest of logos through to the most complex of maps, diagrams and illustrations. Illustrator provides a rich array of tools and commands for creating compelling, distinctive graphics for print, presentations and the Web.

This chapter introduces the fundamentals of the working environment. It covers page setup, the Toolbox, the Windows and Macintosh working environments, and a number of conventions and techniques that will help you to work smoothly and efficiently in Adobe Illustrator.

Covers

Chapter One

Vector v Bitmap

Adobe Illustrator is an object-oriented, vector based drawing application.

Object-oriented means that each shape you create in Illustrator exists as a complete, distinct entity. Even if an object is completely obscured by another object, it still exists and is part of the document.

Vector based means that the shapes or paths you create in Illustrator are defined by mathematical formulae. One significant advantage of this is that if you import an EPS file created in Illustrator into a page layout application such as Adobe InDesign or QuarkXPress, you can enlarge it without losing any quality – lines and curves still print smoothly and crisply. Illustrations created in Illustrator are termed "resolution-independent".

Vector illustration at actual size

Scaled to 400%

This is what makes Adobe Illustrator good for creating artwork consisting of clear-cut, well defined shapes and type effects, as you often find in logos and diagrams.

In contrast, applications such as Adobe Photoshop are pixel based. Images scanned into Photoshop, created from scratch within Photoshop, or captured by a digital camera, consist of a rectangular grid of pixels. So, for example, in Photoshop a circle created on the background layer is not an independent, separate, complete shape – it is the pixels in that area of the grid colored to look like a circle.

Bitmap images are resolution dependent. This means that if you scale up bitmap images they tend to produce jagged, "blocky" output.

Bitmap images are best for images which represent subtle transitions of shade and color as you find in continuous tone images such as photographs.

300ppi (pixels per inch) bitmap image at actual size

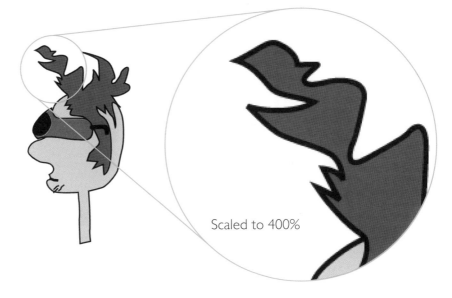

Scaled to 400%

The Illustrator Screen Environment

When you launch Illustrator, the Illustrator application window appears. Along the right-hand side of the window the various Illustrator palettes appear in their default positions. The Toolbox appears along the left edge of the window. To start working in a new document, choose File>New. (See page 14 for further information on using the New Document dialog box.)

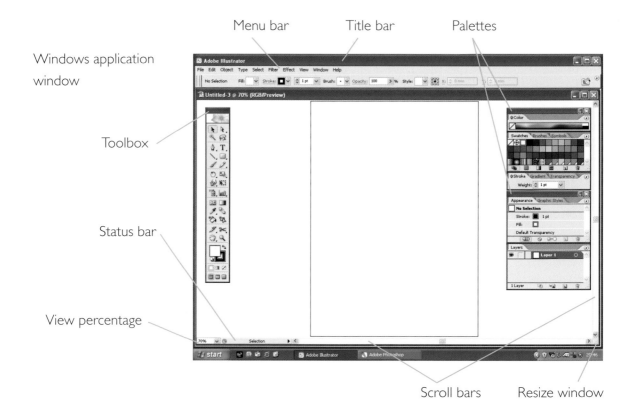

Menu bar   Title bar   Palettes

Windows application window

Toolbox

Status bar

View percentage

Scroll bars   Resize window

Windows v Mac

This book uses a mixture of Windows and Macintosh screen shots and the instructions given apply equally to both platforms. The functionality of Adobe Illustrator on the Windows and Macintosh platforms is virtually identical as an examination of both application windows shows and as you can see from a comparison of the various Windows and Mac dialog boxes throughout the book.

Macintosh application window

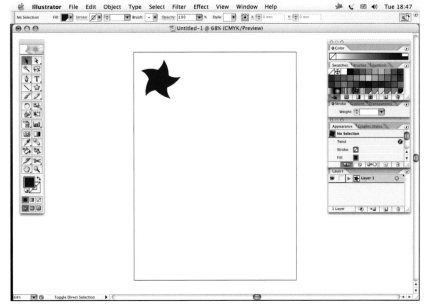

Command (often referred to as "Apple" on the Mac) and Ctrl (Windows) – and Alt/option (Mac) and Alt (Windows) – are used identically as modifier keys. Shift is standard on both platforms.

This book uses Alt/option, with an uppercase "A", to denote both the Macintosh and Windows key of that name.

At the very bottom of the Toolbox are three icons that allow you to control the overall appearance of the Illustrator window:

1 To change from Standard Screen mode to Full Screen Mode with Menu Bar click the Full Screen Mode with Menu Bar button. Here you see a full screen window with a menu bar, but no title bar or scroll bars.

Choose Window> Workspace> Default to return palettes to their default arrangement – the arrangement you see when you launch Illustrator for the first time.

2 Click the Full Screen Mode button to go to Full Screen Mode. Here you see a full screen window, but with no title bar, menu bar or scroll bars.

3 Click the Standard Screen Mode button to go back to Standard Screen mode. Here you see a standard window with a menu bar along the top and scroll bars along the right and bottom edges. Standard Screen mode is the default view shown in these screen shots.

Toolbox Techniques

There are a number of useful general techniques that relate to choosing tools in the Toolbox, including those from the expanded range of hidden tool pop-ups.

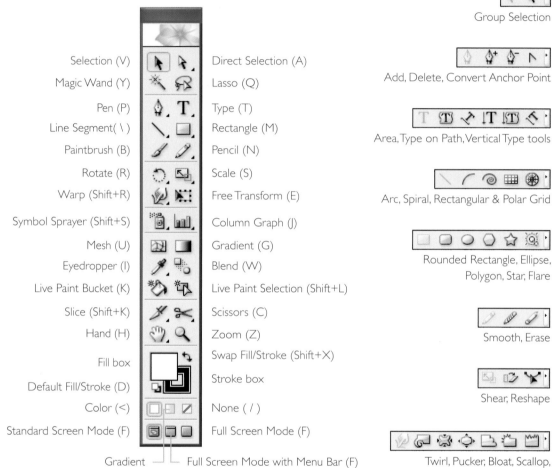

Selection (V)	Direct Selection (A)
Magic Wand (Y)	Lasso (Q)
Pen (P)	Type (T)
Line Segment(\ )	Rectangle (M)
Paintbrush (B)	Pencil (N)
Rotate (R)	Scale (S)
Warp (Shift+R)	Free Transform (E)
Symbol Sprayer (Shift+S)	Column Graph (J)
Mesh (U)	Gradient (G)
Eyedropper (I)	Blend (W)
Live Paint Bucket (K)	Live Paint Selection (Shift+L)
Slice (Shift+K)	Scissors (C)
Hand (H)	Zoom (Z)
Fill box	Swap Fill/Stroke (Shift+X)
Default Fill/Stroke (D)	Stroke box
Color (<)	None (/)
Standard Screen Mode (F)	Full Screen Mode (F)

Gradient —   — Full Screen Mode with Menu Bar (F)

Group Selection

Add, Delete, Convert Anchor Point

Area, Type on Path, Vertical Type tools

Arc, Spiral, Rectangular & Polar Grid

Rounded Rectangle, Ellipse, Polygon, Star, Flare

Smooth, Erase

Shear, Reshape

Twirl, Pucker, Bloat, Scallop, Crystallize, Wrinkle

Stacked Column, Bar, Stacked Bar, Line, Area, Scatter, Pie, Radar

Symbol: Shifter, Scruncher, Sizer, Spinner, Stainer, Screener, Styler

Reflect   Measure   Slice Selection   Knife   Page

1   To choose a tool, click on the tool to select it. The tool highlights. When you position your cursor on the page the cursor icon changes to indicate the tool you selected.

2   A small triangle in the bottom right corner of a tool icon indicates that there are additional tools available in the tool group. To access additional tools, press and hold on the default tool to show the tool pop-up. Move your cursor onto one of the additional

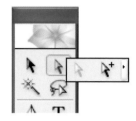

tools then release to select that tool. The tool you select becomes the default tool and appears in the main Toolbox until you make another choice from the tool group.

Rest your cursor on a tool for a few seconds to see the tool tip label which tells you the name of the tool and its keyboard shortcut:

3   Press the keyboard shortcut key on the keyboard to access a tool. To cycle through the additional tools in a tool group, hold down Shift and press the keyboard shortcut key until you reach the tool you want.

4   You can create a tear-off palette for any of the tool groups. Press and hold on a tool group, move your

cursor onto the small triangle in the bar that appears to the right of the tool group. Drag this bar to create a separate tear-off palette of the tools. Reposition this palette as you would for any other palette. Click the Close button in the tear-off palette to close the tear-off.

Even after you create a tear-off palette, you can still access all the tools from the main Toolbox if you want to.

New Document Setup

The maximum artboard size is 227" x 227".

Once you've launched Illustrator, you can set up a new document. You use the New Document dialog box to define the artboard size, and to choose either CMYK or RGB color as the color mode in which you want to work. You can also suggest a name for the file.

Choose CMYK color if you intend your artwork to be color separated and printed on a commercial printing press using process (CMYK) inks. Choose RGB if you intend your artwork to be used on the World Wide Web or in other screen-based presentations.

1 Choose File>New. Enter a name for the new document in the Name field. This is optional at this stage. You can create the new document, then do a Save as to name the file and specify where you want to save it.

2 Choose a Color Mode. Use CMYK Color if your final artwork file is destined for commercial printing using process or spot color inks. Choose RGB Color for images which are destined for the Web or screen based presentation.

Most printers cannot print right to the very edge of the paper. The area that cannot be printed to is called the printer margin, or the non-imageable area. Choose View>Show Page Tiling to see the dotted line representing the printer margin if it is not already showing.

3 Enter Width and Height values to define the size of the Artboard. The Artboard is the overall working area for your document. It is not necessarily the page size of the document, and can be larger than the physical paper size on which you intend to print. OK the dialog box. The solid black rectangle that appears in the center of your screen area represents the size of the artboard. The dotted, inner rectangle defines the printer margin, depending on the current, default printer.

4 To make changes to the artboard size, choose File>Document Setup. Use the Size pop-up to change the artboard to a standard page size, or enter custom width and height dimensions in the Width/Height entry boxes.

5 Use the Units pop-up to choose the unit of measurement for the document.

6 To change the unit of measurement for all subsequently created Illustrator files, choose Edit> Preferences>Units & Display Performance (Windows), or Illustrator>Preferences>Units & Display Performance (Mac). Choose an option from the General pop-up.

The area outside the artboard is referred to as the Scratch area. This extends from the edge of the artboard to the edge of the maximum 227"x227" dimensions. Objects placed on the scratch area are visible on screen, but do not print.

Magnification and Scrolling

The Navigator palette together with the Zoom tool, Hand tool, and the Scroll bars enable you to move precisely to any part of your illustration and to zoom in and out on different portions of the illustration.

1 Choose Window>
Navigator to show
the Navigator
palette. Double-click
the zoom % entry
field to highlight
the existing figure,
enter a new value
(4 – 6400%), then
press Enter/Return
to specify a zoom
level. Alternatively,

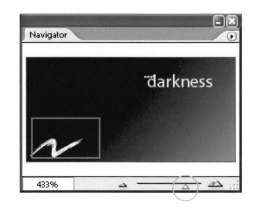

drag the zoom slider to the right to zoom in, to the left to zoom
out. You can also click the small/large mountain buttons to change
the zoom level in preset increments.

2 Each time you change the zoom level, the size
of the Proxy Preview box updates to indicate
the area of the illustration that you have
zoomed in on. Position your cursor in the red
Proxy box, then drag the box to move quickly

to different parts of the page, maintaining the same zoom level.

3 To use the Zoom tool, select it, position your cursor on the image
and click to zoom in on the area around where you clicked, in
preset increments. With the zoom tool selected, hold down Alt/
option. The cursor changes to the zoom out cursor. Click to zoom
out in preset increments.

...cont'd

With any tool, other than the Zoom tool selected, hold down Spacebar+Ctrl/Command to temporarily access the Zoom tool. Add Alt/option to the above combination to zoom out.

4 Another extremely useful technique, with the Zoom tool selected, position your cursor on the illustration, then click and drag to define the area

you want to zoom in on. The smaller the zoom area you define, the greater the resulting magnification.

5 The View menu offers four standard options for changing the magnification of the page. The keyboard shortcut is listed with each option.

Zoom In	Ctrl++
Zoom Out	Ctrl+-
Fit in Window	Ctrl+0
Actual Size	Ctrl+1

6 Use the pop-up menu in the bottom left corner of the Illustrator screen to access the preset magnification increments. Choose a magnification from the list. Or, double-click the value in the Zoom percentage box to highlight the existing value, enter a new zoom value then press Enter/Return to apply it.

With any tool other than the Hand tool selected, hold down Spacebar to temporarily access the Hand tool.

7 In addition to using standard scroll bar techniques to see different parts of an illustration, you can use the Hand tool. Select the Hand tool, position your cursor in the illustration, then click and drag to change the view.

1. The Working Environment   17

Palette Techniques

There are over 26 floating palettes available in Adobe Illustrator. These moveable palettes appear in front of the artwork you create on your Illustrator page. Most of the palettes are initially organized into different groups. You can customize palette groupings to suit our own needs. Use the following techniques to work effectively with palettes.

This section uses Macintosh and Windows screen shots to indicate the identical functionality of the application on both platforms.

1 Use the Window menu to show any palette not already showing. Choosing a particular palette shows the palette along with any other palettes initially grouped with it.

2 To close a palette either use the Window menu and select the appropriate palette command. A checkmark next to a palette name indicates the palette is showing. Or, click the Close button in the title bar of the palette.

3 To move a palette group or an individual palette, position your cursor in the title bar, then click and drag.

4 To make a particular palette active, click the appropriate tab just below the title bar.

5 Drag a tab out of the palette to convert the palette into a standalone palette.

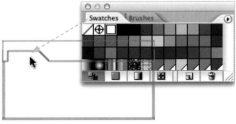

...cont'd

Press the Tab key to hide/show all currently visible palettes including the Toolbox. Hold down Shift, then press Tab to hide/show all currently visible palettes except the Toolbox.

6 Drag a tab into another palette group or individual palette to create a new custom palette group. Drag a palette tab onto the bottom edge of another palette to dock the palette onto the bottom of the other palette.

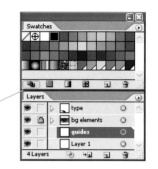

7 To make the most of your available screen space you can shrink and roll up palettes. Click the Minimize button (Windows), or the Zoom button (Mac), in the title bar of the palette. Click the same button to restore the palette to its original size. Double-click a tab to collapse a default size palette (one that has not been resized) to show title bar and tabs only. Double-click a tab to restore a resized palette to its original size.

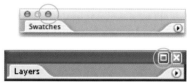

8 You can use standard Mac and Windows techniques to resize some of the palettes, for example the Swatches palette. Click and drag the resize icon for the palette.

9 Most of the palettes in Illustrator have a palette menu which contains a range of commands and options relevant to the active palette. Click on the palette menu button (⊙) to show the palette menu.

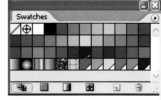

Ruler Guides

Ruler Guides are non-printing guides that enable you to align elements in an illustration accurately and precisely. Make sure that you have page rulers showing in order to create ruler guides. Choose View>Show Rulers (Ctrl/Command+R) if the rulers are not already showing.

Drawing tool cursors snap to guides when they come within 2 pixels of a guide. This helps ensure that you create objects precisely and accurately. Also, as you move an object, when the Move cursor comes within 2 pixels of a guide it snaps onto it. The cursor turns hollow to indicate that it has snapped to the guide.

When you use the Lock Guides command you are locking/unlocking all ruler guides in the document.

1 To create a ruler guide, position your cursor in either the top or left ruler, then click and drag onto your page. Release the mouse button.

2 By default, ruler guides are locked as soon as you create them. To reposition a guide, choose View>Guides>Lock Guides (Ctrl/Command+Alt/option+;). The tick mark indicates that Lock Guides is on. By selecting the option you are switching off Lock Guides. Position your cursor on the guide, then click and drag.

3 To remove a guide, make sure that the guides are unlocked, then using the Selection tool, click on the guide to select. Press the Backspace or Delete key to delete it.

4 To temporarily hide ruler guides, choose View>Guides>Hide Guides (Ctrl/Command+;). Choose View>Guides>Show Guides to redisplay hidden guides. To remove all ruler guides, choose View>Guides>Clear Guides.

Hide Guides	Ctrl+;
Lock Guides	Alt+Ctrl+;
Make Guides	Ctrl+5
Release Guides	Alt+Ctrl+5
Clear Guides	

Use the keyboard shortcut, Ctrl/Command+5 to make an object into a guide; Ctrl/Command+Alt/option+5 to release a selected guide so that it becomes an object again.

5 Be very careful if you have unlocked guides, then use a marquee select technique to select objects that are positioned next to ruler guides. Unlocked ruler guides can be selected along with the objects you marquee. If you then reposition or delete the selected objects, the guides are also affected. This can sometimes be desirable, sometimes not.

6 You can turn any path into a guide. Select an object you want to convert into a guide. Choose View>Guides>Make Guide.

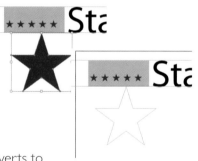

7 To release the guide so that it reverts to an object, first unlock guides, click on the guide you want to release, then choose View>Guides>Release Guides. Any original fill and stroke attributes are restored.

8 To set preferences for the appearance and color of Ruler Guides choose Edit>Preferences>Guides and Grid (Windows), or Illustrator> Preferences>Guides and Grid (Mac).

Paths, Points and Selection Tools

There are three selection tools in Adobe Illustrator – the Selection tool, the Direct Selection tool and the Group Selection tool. An important part of understanding Adobe Illustrator is to understand how and why to use each tool.

Equally fundamental is understanding paths and points. Chapter Ten covers working with Paths and Points in detail. But a brief introduction is necessary at the outset.

This section provides an overview of the functionality of each Selection tool and indicates where you can find further information and practical examples of using the tools.

Paths

Every object that you create in Adobe Illustrator, with the exception of type, has a path. A path can be open or closed and consists of at least two anchor points, joined together by either straight line segments or curve segments, or a combination of both. The path defines the shape of the object.

You can fill paths with a color, a gradient or pattern and you can also stroke the path. A stroke is a color and thickness applied to the path itself and acts as an outline on the path.

The Selection tool

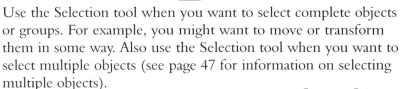

Use the Selection tool when you want to select complete objects or groups. For example, you might want to move or transform them in some way. Also use the Selection tool when you want to select multiple objects (see page 47 for information on selecting multiple objects).

Existing Illustrator users may not like the bounding box. To switch off the bounding box choose Edit>Preferences> General (Windows), or Illustrator> Preferences>General (Mac). Deselect the Use Bounding Box option.

When you click on an object with the Selection tool a bounding box with eight selection handles appears around the object. Also, the anchor points that define the shape of the path appear as solid squares.

The Direct Selection tool

Use the Direct Selection tool when you want to select individual anchor points or path segments that help define the shape of

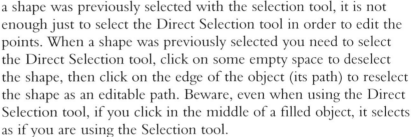

an object in order to edit them. You can also select multiple points (see page 152 for information on selecting and editing points). When you select an individual point it appears as a solid square. Non-selected points appear as hollow squares.

You have to be very precise about the way you use the Direct Selection tool. If a shape was previously selected with the selection tool, it is not enough just to select the Direct Selection tool in order to edit the points. When a shape was previously selected you need to select the Direct Selection tool, click on some empty space to deselect the shape, then click on the edge of the object (its path) to reselect the shape as an editable path. Beware, even when using the Direct Selection tool, if you click in the middle of a filled object, it selects as if you are using the Selection tool.

Selected anchor points appear as solid squares, unselected anchor points are hollow.

The Group Selection tool

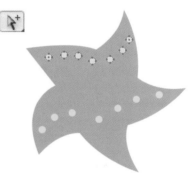

Use the Group Selection tool to select one, or all, of the objects in a group. The Group Selection tool also enables you to work with groups grouped with other groups in a grouping hierarchy (see page 78 for further information). Illustrator graphs are initially created as a hierarchy of groups and the Group Selection tool is an important tool if you want to be able to continue to edit the data used to create the chart (see Chapter Twelve).

The Lasso tool

The Lasso tool allows you to drag in a freeform manner to create an irregular selection area. Either drag around the outside of an object to select all anchor points on the object, or drag around an area to select specific anchor points within the area you define.

Preview and Outline

Most of the time as you build an illustration you work in Preview mode. In Preview you see objects partially or fully according to their stacking order and with their fill color and stroke attributes. In Outline mode, you see a wireframe view of all the paths in the illustration.

As illustrations become increasingly complex, Outline mode can be very useful for selecting objects that are difficult to select in Preview and to troubleshoot problems which are difficult to identify in Preview mode. Screen redraw is also quicker in Outline mode, especially when working with complex illustrations.

1 To change from Preview to Outline and vice versa, choose View>Outline/Preview (Ctrl/Command+Y).

2 You can select and manipulate objects in Outline view using the Selection tool, but you must click on the edge of the shape. If you click inside a shape you do not select it.

3 Another technique for selecting objects obscured by other objects, making them difficult to select, is to use the context menu. Select an object using the Selection tool, then click the right mouse button (Windows) or hold down control then click the mouse button (Mac). Choose a command from the Select sub-menu in the context sensitive menu that appears.

Undo Move	
Redo	
Group	
Join	
Average...	
Make Clipping Mask	
Make Compound Path	
Make Guides	
Transform	▶
Arrange	▶
Select	▶ First Object Above
	Next Object Above
	Next Object Below
	Last Object Below

Saving Views

If you need to return to a particular part of an illustration at a particular zoom level, you can create a New View. When you want to return to that particular view you simply use the View menu to choose the view you want.

1   To create a new view, use any of the magnification and scroll techniques to get to a view of your illustration that you want to return to quickly and easily whenever you need to.

2   Choose View>New View. Enter a name for the view, and OK the dialog box.

New View

Name: [pit wheel] [OK] [Cancel]

3   To return to exactly the same view, go to the View menu, then select the name of the view from the bottom of the menu.

New View...
Edit Views...

pit wheel
moon
river

4   To edit a view, choose View>Edit View. Click on the view you want to edit. Either change the name of the view in the Name entry field, or click the Delete button to delete the view.

Edit Views

pit wheel
moon
river

Name: [river]

[OK] [Cancel] [Delete]

Undoing Mistakes

One of the most essential techniques in Adobe Illustrator is undoing a mistake when something goes wrong and you need to step back one or two moves.

The number of undos you can perform is unlimited, being restricted only by the amount of memory (RAM) available on your system.

The Undo command will work even after you have used the Save command.

1 To correct a mistake, choose Edit>Undo (Ctrl/Command+Z). The Undo command is dimmed if you cannot undo an operation.

Edit	
Undo Move	Ctrl+Z
Redo Move	Shift+Ctrl+Z

2 Choose Edit>Redo (Ctrl/Command+Shift+Z) to reverse through any undos.

3 Using the Status bar pop-up menu, you can choose Number of Undos from the Show sub-menu to display a readout of the number of Undos available. There is no fixed limit to the number of undos you can perform. It depends on how much memory is available on your computer system.

Versions…		Version Cue Status
Alternates…		Current Tool
		Date and Time
Reveal in Bridge…		✔ Number of Undos
Show	▶	Document Color Profile

97 Undos; 3 Redos ▶ ◀

97 Undos; 3 Redos ▶ ◀

You cannot undo the File>Revert command.

4 To revert to the last saved version of a file, choose File>Revert. Confirm "Revert" in the warning dialog box. The file reverts to the stage it was at when you last used the Save command. This can sometimes be more efficient than using repeated undo commands.

Adobe Illustrator

⚠ Revert to saved version of the Adobe Illustrator document "pathspoints.ai"?

[Revert] [Cancel]

Open, Place, Save and Print Files

Adobe Illustrator can open files created in Illustrator itself as well as from a wide variety of other applications. You can also place or import files into an existing Illustrator file. Placed files can be either linked (the file remains external to the Illustrator file and Illustrator remembers a link to the file) or embedded (the complete file information for the placed file is included in the Illustrator file).

This chapter also covers saving files in Illustrator EPS format, using the Save for Web dialog box and basic printing techniques.

Covers

Chapter Two

Opening Files in Adobe Illustrator

Illustrator offers a wide variety of options for opening files. You can open Illustrator files saved in Illustrator format, Illustrator EPS format and Adobe PDF format.

You can also open files created in other applications such as Adobe Photoshop. When you open a file created by another application it is converted into a new Adobe Illustrator file. Vector artwork in the file you open is converted into Illustrator paths. Bitmap images remain in bitmap format.

PDF (Portable Document Format) files can be opened as Adobe Illustrator documents. PDF files can represent both vector and bitmap information. You can edit artwork with Illustrator tools and commands.

1 To open a file, choose File>Open.

2 Use standard Windows/ Macintosh dialog boxes to navigate to the location of the file you want to open.

3 Click on the file name to select it, then click the Open button. Alternatively, double-click the file name.

4 Or, choose File>Open Recent, then select a file from the list of recently opened files.

1 circlespdf.pdf
2 cd-wallet-01.ai
3 redglasses.ai
4 cartoonhead.eps
5 cartoonfigures.tif
6 DVD Slip Sheet.ait
7 CD Label.ait
8 starguides.ai
9 pathspoints.ai
10 cd-cover-01.ai

5 Click the Use Adobe Dialog button to navigate to and open files using an Adobe variation of the Open dialog box. This Adobe Open dialog box is standard across applications in Adobe Creative Suite 2 and provides a consistent file management interface across Windows and Macintosh platforms.

Adobe Bridge

Click the Favorites tab, then click Bridge Center to display the main Adobe Bridge window if necessary.

Adobe Bridge provides a central interface for organizing, locating, tracking and managing your files. It provides file management facilities which are consistent across all applications in the Adobe Creative Suite 2, helping to streamline file management tasks.

1 To open the Bridge from within Adobe Illustrator, click the Go to Bridge button located in the far right of the Control palette.

You can launch Adobe Bridge as a standalone application, as you would launch any other application – from the Start>Programs menu in Windows, or from the Applications folder on the Mac.

2 Click the Adobe Stock Photos panel to search online for images from stock photo libraries. A search area opens where you can enter keywords or Image IDs to begin your search.

3 The Recent Folders pane lists the most recent folders used by Creative Suite applications on your computer. Click a folder icon to display the contents.

To create a file group, make sure only files you want to include are open in their respective applications. Click the Save open files into a file group option. In the Adobe Bridge dialog box, enter a name for the file group. OK the dialog box:

SAVED FILE GROUPS

Files that are open within the suite applications can be closed and saved as a group. Opening the group will re-open the files in the respective applications.

Save open files into a file group.

dvd-cover-02
6/3/05, 10:7 AM

4 The Recent Files pane lists the most recent files used by applications on your computer. Click a file icon to open the file. If the appropriate application is not running, Bridge launches it and opens the file so that you can work on it.

To open a project of related files previously saved as a file group, click the file group folder icon in the list then click in the Open this file group panel.

5 If you are working with files in different applications which are part of the same project, and the files are currently open, you can use Bridge to create a file group. This brings together the related files and makes it easy to manage, locate and track all the related files in a project.

Folder and File Browser View

Click the Folders tab to view, manage, sort and open files on your hard disk. You can also use the Folder view to create new folders and to rename, move, delete and rank files.

Choose an option from the View>Sort sub-menu to control the way image thumbnails are ordered in the Preview pane:

1 In the Adobe Bridge window, click the Folder tab. Use the Folder panel to navigate to specific folders on your hard disk using standard Windows/Macintosh techniques. You can also use the Look in drop down list, to navigate quickly to recently used folders.

2 The content area on the right of the window displays thumbnail previews of the contents of the selected folder. Drag the Thumbnail Size

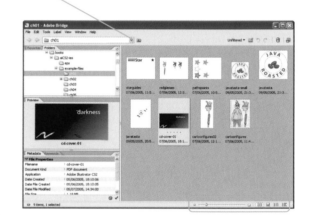

slider to control the size of thumbnail previews in the contents area. Use the View buttons to control their arrangement.

To move a file, position your cursor on the image thumbnail, then drag it to a different folder in the Folder panel of the Adobe Bridge window. To copy a file to a new location, hold down Alt/option, then drag it to a different folder.

3 File information for a selected image file appears in the Metadata and Keyword palettes. With the Metadata tab selected, click the expand triangle to the left of Camera Data (Exif) to view image information imported from a digital camera.

4 To open a file from the content area, click on an image thumbnail to select it, then press the Enter/Return key. You can also double-click a thumbnail.

5 To delete a file, click on the file thumbnail to select it, then either click the Wastebasket icon in the Bridge Toolbar, or drag the file onto the Wastebasket. Alternatively, you can press the Delete key.

To display thumbnails in the content area according to their rank, choose View>Sort>By Rating:

6 To create a 1–5 star ranking for an image, click the leftmost dot below the thumbnail to convert it to a star. To remove a star, click the star to the left of the final star.

7 To display only thumbnails with a specific star rating or higher, select an option from the Filter pop-up menu.

8 Click the Metadata or Keywords tab to view additional labeling information saved with an image. You can also use options from the palette menu for each tab to add and edit metadata and keyword information for your image files. Use the Expand/Collapse triangle to display/hide information for each category.

An open file icon appears with the thumbnail if the image is already open in an application:

9 To run a slide show for images in a folder, choose View>Slide Show. Use the Adobe Bridge Slide Show panel to control the slide show. Press H on the keyboard to hide or show the Slide Show commands panel.

Saving in Illustrator Format

Save a file in Illustrator format when you want to open the file in Adobe Illustrator, place the file into an application which accepts Illustrator format, such as Adobe Photoshop and Adobe InDesign, or to create an Illustrator file that is compatible with earlier versions of Illustrator.

Leave the Append File Extension and Lower Case options selected. This is especially useful and important if your artwork is likely to be used on the World Wide Web.

As with any other software application, it is good practice to save a new, untitled file at an early stage. Use the Save as command to specify where you want to save the file and to give it a name.

1 To save an untitled file, choose File> Save as.

2 Use standard Windows/ Macintosh dialog boxes to specify the folder into which you want to save the file.

3 Drag across the existing text in the File Name box, if necessary, to highlight it, then enter a name for the file.

(Windows) When you save in Adobe Illustrator format, the first time you click the Save button, Illustrator appends the .ai file extension. Click the Save button again to proceed.

4 The default format is set to Illustrator. Click the Save button.

5 In the Illustrator Options dialog box use the Version pop-up to choose a compatibility option. Leave Version set to Illustrator CS2 unless you want to make the file compatible with earlier versions of Illustrator. If you

Use the File>Save a Copy command to save a copy of the current file (Illustrator automatically adds the word "copy" to the file name). This leaves the original file as the active file, so you can continue to work with it.

choose to make the file compatible with earlier versions of Illustrator, new features, not available in the earlier version, are not retained. For example, Gradient Mesh objects cannot be saved in Illustrator v6 format.

6 Reduce the Subset Font % value only if you need to keep file size to an absolute minimum. Enter a value lower than 100% to set a threshold value to specify when a font subset is created. When the percentage of font characters used in the document exceeds the threshold, the complete font information saves with the file, otherwise only the characters used in the document are saved.

Use the Save command (Ctrl/ Command+S) regularly to save changes you make to the illustration. Then, if there is any kind of system failure or crash, you can restart your computer and reopen the file at the stage it was at when you did your last save.

7 If you want to embed linked images you have placed within the file you are saving, select the Include Linked Files option. This option is only available if you have placed files in the Illustration (see page 38).

Transparency options only affect your artwork if you save in Illustrator 8, or earlier, file format.

8 Leave the Create PDF Compatible File checkbox selected to ensure that the Illustrator file is compatible with other Adobe applications. Deselect the Embed ICC Profiles checkbox if you do not want to create color-managed document. Use Compression compresses PDF data in the document. Deselect this checkbox only if it considerably slows down the time it takes a file to save to disk.

Saving in Illustrator EPS Format

Save a file in Illustrator EPS (Encapsulated PostScript) format when you want to place it in another application such as QuarkXPress or Adobe InDesign. The majority of page layout, word-processing and graphics applications allow you to import or place EPS files, making this a very versatile format.

1 Follow steps 1–3, Saving in Illustrator Format (page 32), but then choose Illustrator EPS from the Save as Type pop-up

| Adobe Illustrator (*.AI) |
| Adobe PDF (*.PDF) |
| Illustrator EPS (*.EPS) |
| Illustrator Template (*.AIT) |
| SVG (*.SVG) |
| SVG Compressed (*.SVGZ) |

(Windows), or Format pop-up (Mac). When you save a file in EPS format in Windows, the .eps file extension is automatically added to the file name. Click the Save button.

2 Choose a different Version option only if you need to make your Illustrator file compatible with earlier versions of Illustrator.

3 Choose a Preview Format option. Preview refers to the on-screen preview of the EPS file which you see when you import it into another application. The 8-bit options give the best preview, but increase the overall size of the EPS file. Choose an IBM PC or Macintosh preview depending on which platform you will use the

Choose Opaque as the background option for an 8-bit TIFF preview if you intend to place the EPS in a Microsoft Office application.

file. Transparent/Opaque options become available when you choose an 8-bit color TIFF preview. Select Transparent to create a transparent background for the preview image when it is placed in another application. Opaque gives a solid background.

4 For an Illustrator CS/ CS2 file which includes transparency effects or overprinting colors, use the Overprints pop-up to either preserve or discard overprint settings in the document; use the Preset pop-up to choose a Flattener setting which controls how transparent effects are treated. Choose the High Resolution preset for best quality results.

To prevent the illegal use of fonts, Illustrator only embeds fonts in a document that are properly licensed.

5 Leave the Embed Fonts checkbox selected to include fonts used in the document as part of the file.

6 Select the Include Linked Files checkbox to embed complete file information for placed images linked to the file you are saving. Selecting this option increases the size of the EPS file.

7 Select the Include Document Thumbnails checkbox if you want to see a preview of the file in Illustrator's Open and Place dialog boxes.

You should read any warning prompts in the Warnings area at the bottom of the EPS Options dialog box. The warning prompts often contain useful information which can help you avoid potential pitfalls.

8 Select the Include CMYK PostScript checkbox to convert RGB colors used in the file to their CMYK equivalents if you print the EPS from an application which does not support RGB output.

9 Use the Adobe PostScript pop-up to specify the PostScript format for the file. Make sure you choose PostScript Language Level 3 if you have included gradient mesh objects in the file and you are printing to a PostScript Level 3 printer. This helps ensure efficient printing for such objects.

Save for Web

The Save for Web dialog box enables you to save vector artwork created in Illustrator in a bitmap file format (.gif, .jpg and .png) suitable for use on the World Wide Web or in other on-screen presentations. Establishing an optimal balance between file size and image quality – optimization – is the central issue when saving files for such purposes.

Click the 4-Up tab to see representations of the Original image, the Optimized image and two other, lower quality variations of the current optimization settings.

1   Choose File>Save to save any changes to the original Illustrator artwork. Then choose File>Save for Web.

2   Click the 2-Up tab to see the original image side by side with the image as it appears with the current optimization settings applied to it. The annotations area at the bottom of the palette displays useful information, including file format, size and approximate download time for the image.

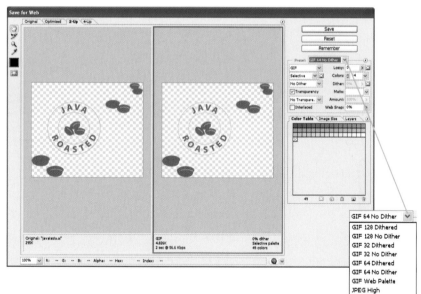

If you click into an optimization pane, the pane becomes active, indicated by a black border on the pane. When you OK the dialog box, the version of the image in the active pane is saved.

3   Choose a preset optimization setting from those available in the Presets pop-up. The fields in the Optimization area of the dialog box update automatically, as does the preview in the Optimized image pane.

4 Use the Download pop-up menu to choose a modem speed. The estimated download time in the annotations area changes depending on the speed you choose.

5 Click Save when you are satisfied. Use the Save Optimized As dialog box to specify a name and location for the file. The file extension is added automatically and depends on the optimization setting chosen. Be careful not to delete the file extension if you change the name of the file.

6 Select Save HTML and Images option from the Save as Type pop-up (Windows), Format pop-up (Mac), if you want Illustrator to generate an additional HTML file with the image. You can open the HTML file in your browser to evaluate the results of the settings you specified. The file is named automatically and saved into the same folder as the optimized image.

Placing Files

You can place, or import, files created in other applications into your Adobe Illustrator artwork. Placed files can either be linked (the file remains external to the Illustrator file), or embedded (the complete file information is included in the Illustrator file).

1 To place a file, choose File>Place. Use standard Windows/Macintosh dialog boxes to navigate to the file you want to place. Click on a file name to select it. If available, a preview appears in the Preview box.

2 Deselect the Link checkbox to include the full placed file information in the Illustrator file, adding to the file size of the Illustrator document. The embedded file icon appears with the file name in the Links palette. Select the Link checkbox to create a link between the image and the Illustrator file. The image is not embedded in the Illustrator file, keeps the file size of the Illustrator document smaller. Use the Links palette to monitor and update the status of placed and embedded files.

3 Select the Template checkbox to place a file on a new, non-printing layer. A dimmed representation of the image appears on the template layer. You cannot select, move or otherwise manipulate it without first unlocking the layer.

4 Click the Place button when you are satisfied with the options you have selected. The image is placed into Illustrator and is initially selected. Provided that the placed file was saved with an appropriate preview, the placed image file always displays in Preview view.

Managing Links

Use the Links palette (Window>Links) to manage linked files within Illustrator. The Links palette lists all linked and embedded images. Linked files appear as a thumbnail and name. A question mark icon next to a linked image indicates that the original file has been moved or is missing. An embedded file is indicated by the generic objects icon.

I To display link information, click on a file in the Links palette, then choose Information from the palette menu (⊙). You can also double-click a placed file name in the Links palette.

2 To update a link, select a linked file that has been modified since it was placed. Either click the Update Link button (🖫→) in the bottom of the palette, or choose Update Link from the palette menu.

3 To relink to a missing file, click on the linked file entry in the palette. Either, click the Relink button (⬚→), or choose Relink from the palette menu. Locate the file you want, click on the file name to select it, then click Place.

4 If a linked file is moved from its current location on the hard disk, when you next open your Illustrator file a Warning box indicates that the link is missing. Click the Repair button, then navigate to the file to relink to it. Click Replace to replace the missing file with a different image. Click the Ignore button to open the Illustrator file without relinking to the missing placed file.

Printing Basics

When you complete an illustration, or at various stages as you build it, you will need to print a copy for proofing purposes. The Illustrator Print dialog box provides a comprehensive set of printing controls for printing a basic composite proof – where all colors print on the same sheet of paper, through to controls for printing separations suitable for commercial printing. The following steps show you how to print a basic, composite proof copy of your artwork.

1 To print a copy of your artwork, choose File>Print.

2 Use the Printer pop-up menu to select the printer you want to use.

3 In the General area of the Print dialog box, enter the number of copies you want to print. Specify a page range if there is more than 1 page in the document.

If you want to reuse the same set of Illustrator print settings on a regular basis it is worth saving the settings as a preset. To do this, create the settings you require in the Illustrator Print dialog box, then click the Save Preset button to give the settings a name. The next time you access the Print dialog box you can select the print preset from the Print Preset pop-up menu.

4 In the Media area, choose a paper size from the Size pop-up menu and also choose an orientation option. As you select different orientation options the pint preview box on the left of the dialog box updates to represent the results visually.

Click the Setup button at the bottom of the Print dialog box to access the printer specific Print dialog box for the selected printer. Refer to the printer manufacturer's manuals for detailed information on the options available for your printer.

5 In the Options area use the Print Layers pop-up menu to specify which layers print. If necessary, you can select the Fit to Page radio button to reduce oversize artwork to fit onto the selected paper size, or you can specify custom scale percentages.

6 Click on any of the print control categories in the list on the left hand side of the dialog box to access and set more advanced print settings. For example, you can use the Marks & Bleeds panel to specify additional page marks such as Trim Marks, Crop Marks and Color Bars which are typically used by commercial printers for printing purposes. You can use the Output panel to specify advanced options for creating color separations.

7 Click the Print button when you are ready to print a copy of your Illustrator document.

Crop Areas and Crop Marks

Crop Marks are small lines placed at the corners of a page to indicate where the page is to be trimmed. Illustrator can only create one crop area for an illustration. The Crop Area command creates crop marks around the artboard, or to the dimensions of a selected rectangle. You cannot edit the crop marks created by this command.

You can select, move and manipulate crop marks created using the Filter>Create>Crop Marks option.

To release crop marks, choose Object>Crop Marks>Release. The crop marks are converted into a rectangle the size of the page, with a fill and stroke of none. Delete the rectangle if you have no further use for it.

1 To create a crop area for an entire page, choose Object>Crop Area>Make. Crop marks appear around the corners of the artboard.

2 To create a crop area based on a rectangle, first create a rectangle to define an area of the page. Choose Object>Crop Area>Make. The original rectangle disappears and is replaced by crop marks which can be used to trim the page to the size of the rectangle.

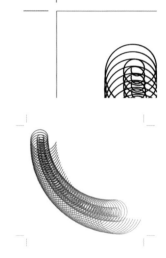

Unlike crop areas, you can select, move and delete crop marks created using the Filter>Create>Crop Marks command.

The Crop Marks Filter

You can create more than one set of crop marks in an illustration by using the Crop Marks command from the Filter menu.

1 To create crop marks, select an object or objects. Choose Filter>Create>Crop Marks. Eight lines – the crop marks – are placed around the selected object(s).

Registration is the color applied automatically to crop marks to ensure that they appear on all plates if you make separations.

2 To delete crop marks, use the Selection tool to select the crop marks then press the Backspace/Delete key.

Basic Shapes and Brushes

Basic shapes such as rectangles and squares, ovals and circles, stars, polygons and lines form the staple of most illustrations created in Adobe Illustrator. This chapter looks at various techniques for creating these basic shapes, and at other basic but essential techniques such as selecting, deselecting, scaling, moving and deleting objects.

The Pencil tool and the Paintbrush tool can be used to create open or closed paths. They both work in a freeform manner as you drag the mouse. The Paintbrush tool works in conjunction with the Brushes palette.

Covers

Chapter Three

Drawing Basic Shapes

By default, objects drawn using the Rectangle and Ellipse tools grow outward from the point at which you start to drag. Objects drawn with the Polygon, Spiral and Star tools grow from their center point outward.

The following drawing techniques can be used with tools such as the Rectangle, Rounded Rectangle, Ellipse, Polygon, Star, Line, Arc and Spiral.

1. To draw basic shapes, select one of the above tools. Position your cursor on the page. The cursor changes to the standard drawing cursor. Click and drag. You can drag in any direction away from the start point. Typically you will drag down and to the right.

In the middle of drawing a basic shape, in other words, before you release the mouse button, hold down the Spacebar if you want to reposition the shape as you draw it.

2. To draw squares and circles, select the Rectangle tool or the Ellipse tool. Position your cursor on the page. Hold down Shift, then click and drag. The shape is constrained to square or circular proportions as long as you hold down the Shift key. Release the mouse button before you release the Shift key.

When you use the Shift key as a constraint, make sure that you release the mouse button before you release the Shift key, otherwise the constraint effect is lost.

3. To constrain polygons and stars, select either the Polygon or Star drawing tool. Position your cursor on the page. Hold down Shift, then click and drag to create the shape. Holding down Shift in this instance ensures that you keep the base of the polygon, or the "legs" of the star, level. Release the mouse button before you release the Shift key.

To draw a square or a circle from the center out, hold down Shift+Alt/option as you drag.

4 To draw rectangles and ellipses from the center out, select a Rectangle or Ellipse drawing tool. Position your cursor on the page. Hold down Alt/option. The cursor changes to the "center out" drawing cursor. Click and drag to create the shape. Release the mouse button before you release the Alt/option key.

5 To delete an object, make sure the object is selected, using the Selection tool, or the Group-selection tool, then choose Edit>Clear, or press the Backspace or Delete key.

After you draw a basic shape, the object remains selected – indicated by the solid anchor points that define the shape of the path. The current fill and stroke attributes are automatically applied to the object. Click away from the object if you want to deselect it:

If you select the Selection tool, a bounding box with 8 selection handles also appears around the object:

Dialog Box Method

When you need precise control over the size of an object, you can use a dialog box to create shapes to exact dimensions.

1 To create a shape to precise dimensions, select a basic shape drawing tool.

2 Position your cursor on the page. Click (do not click and drag). The appropriate dialog box appears.

3 Enter values for Width and Height for rectangles and circles, and a corner radius value for rectangles with rounded corners.

4 For a polygon enter a Radius value. The Radius is the distance from the center point to the end point of each segment that constitutes the polygon. Enter a value for number of sides, or use the increment arrows to increase/decrease the number of sides.

Rectangle
Options
Width: 2 in
Height: 2 in
OK
Cancel

Ellipse
Options
Width: 3 in
Height: 3 in
OK
Cancel

Rounded Rectangle
Options
Width: 2.5 in
Height: 2.5 in
Corner Radius: 0.1667 in
OK
Cancel

Polygon
Options
Radius: 2 in
Sides: 5
OK
Cancel

When you use a drawing tool dialog box, the values initially displayed are those used to create the last shape you drew with that tool.

5 For a star enter Radius 1 and Radius 2 values. The Radius 1 value describes the radius of a circle that defines the inner points in the star; the Radius 2 describes the radius of a circle that defines the position of the outer points of a star. Click the increment arrows to increase or decrease the number of points in the star, or enter a value in the Points entry box.

6 For spirals enter a Radius value. This is the distance from the center point to the outermost point in the spiral. Enter a Decay rate. Decay rate determines the rate of expansion of each successive wind of the spiral. (A wind is one complete turn of the spiral e.g. from the 12 o'clock to 12 o'clock position.) Enter a value for Segments. Illustrator uses 4 segments to create one complete wind of the spiral. Click the clockwise or counterclockwise radio button to determine the direction of the spiral.

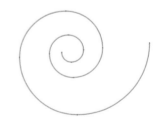

Decay= 70   Decay= 80   Decay= 90

Selecting Multiple Objects

There are three essential techniques for selecting multiple objects. Use the Selection tool (solid arrow) or the Lasso Selection tool when selecting complete objects.

Objects selected using the following techniques form a temporary grouping – moving one object moves all the selected objects whilst maintaining their exact position relative to each other. As soon as you click away from the objects, this temporary grouping is lost.

Selecting all objects

Working with the Selection tool, choose Edit>Select all to select all objects in the illustration. This includes objects on the pasteboard, but not any locked or hidden objects.

Selecting multiple objects with the Shift key

Select the Selection tool. Click on the first object you want to select. Hold down the Shift key, then click on other objects that you want to add to the initial selection.

To "marquee" select multiple objects

Once you have multiple objects selected you can move, fill, transform and manipulate them using any editing tool.

Make sure you have the Selection tool selected if you want to select complete objects. Position your cursor so that it is not on top of any existing object. Click and

drag. A dotted marquee box appears as you drag the mouse. Whatever this dotted rectangle touches will be selected when you release the mouse button. This is an extremely powerful selection technique and is worth practising if it is new to you.

To deselect all objects, you can use the keyboard shortcut: Ctrl/Command+ Shift+A.

2 Use the Lasso Selection tool to create a freeform, non-rectangular selection around objects. This tool can create complex, more precise selections than the previous technique, but takes longer.

Magic Wand Tool

The Magic Wand tool provides efficient options for selecting objects with the same fill color, stroke weight or color, opacity or blending mode. You can use the Magic Wand palette to specify tolerance values, so that you can select objects with similar attributes that fall within the tolerance values you set.

With the Magic Wand tool selected, click on some empty space to deselect all objects in the document.

1 To select objects with the same fill color, select the Magic Wand tool. Click once on an object to select all objects in the document with the same fill color.

2 Hold down Shift, then click on another object to add to the initial selection of objects. All objects with the same attributes as the object you Shift+Click on are added to the initial selection. Hold down Alt/option, then click on an object to remove it, and all other objects with the same fill attributes, from the selection.

If you make a complex selection which you may need again, at a later stage, choose Select>Save Selection. Enter a name for the selection in the Save Selection dialog box, then click OK. To reselect exactly the same objects, choose the name of the saved selection from the bottom of the Select menu.

Creating Custom Magic Wand settings

You can use the Magic Wand palette to create custom settings for the Magic Wand tool.

1 Choose Window>Magic Wand, or double-click the Magic Wand tool, to show the Magic Wand palette. Select or deselect Fill, Stroke, Opacity and Blending Mode checkboxes to include or exclude the attribute as required.

2 Use the Tolerance entry boxes, or drag the Tolerance pop-up slider, to set a tolerance value. Setting a tolerance value allows you to select objects which do not exactly match the initial object on which you click, but which share similar values for the specific attribute. Low tolerance values select a limited range of objects; higher tolerance values select a wider range of objects.

Click the angle bracket button (▶) to the right of the Tolerance entry box to reveal the Tolerance slider.

Resizing Objects

After you draw a basic shape you can resize it manually using the Selection tool. You can also resize groups, open paths, brush strokes and text using the same techniques.

If an object does not have a fill, you must click on its path (the edge) to select it – it does not select if you click inside the shape.

1 To resize a basic shape, select the Selection tool. Select the object or group you want to resize. A bounding box with 8 selection handles appears around the object or group.

2 Drag the center left/right handle to increase/decrease the width of the object. Drag the center top/bottom handle to resize the height. Drag a corner handle to resize width and height simultaneously. As you resize an object Illustrator creates a preview of the new size of the object, indicated by a thin blue preview line. Release when the shape is the required size.

3 To maintain the proportions of an object or group, hold down Shift then drag a selection handle.

To select an individual object within a group, select either the Direct Selection tool or the Group Selection tool, then click on the object. A bounding box with 8 selection handles appears around the object.

4 To scale an object around its center point, hold down Alt/option then drag a selection handle.

Moving Objects

Start to drag an object(s), then hold down Shift to constrain the movement of the object(s) horizontally, vertically, or to increments of 45 degrees.

Depending on your requirements you can move objects visually using the mouse, or precise distances using the Move dialog box or the keyboard.

1   To move an object visually, select the Selection tool. Click on an object to select it. For an object with no fill, position your cursor on the path. For an object with a fill you can position your cursor inside the object. Do not position your cursor on one of the selection handles.

To change the cursor increment, choose Edit> Preferences> General (Windows), or Illustrator> Preferences>General (Mac). Enter a new value in the Keyboard Increment entry box:

2   Click and drag to move the object to a new position. Release the mouse button when the preview, indicated by a blue bounding box, is where you want it.

Moving objects in increments

1   Using the Selection tool, click on an object(s) to select it. Press the up, down, left or right arrow keys on the keyboard to move the object in 1 point (.353 mm) increments.

Moving objects precise distances

1   Using the Selection tool, select an object(s). Choose Object> Transform>Move. In the Move dialog box, either enter values for Horizontal and Vertical, or enter values for Distance and Angle. If you enter values for Horizontal and Vertical, the Distance and Angle values update and vice versa.

Enter positive Horizontal values to move an object to the right. Enter a negative Horizontal value to move an object to the left. Enter a positive Vertical value to move an object upward. Enter a negative Vertical value to move an object downward.

2   Click the Copy button if you want to move a copy of the object(s). The original remains in place and a copy of the object(s) moves to the new position specified.

Cut, Copy, Paste, Clear

Use the Clipboard as a temporary storage area only. If you cut something important to the Clipboard, paste it back into the document as soon as possible to minimize the risk of accidentally overwriting it with another cut or copy action.

The Cut/Copy/Paste commands use the Clipboard as a temporary storage area for objects you create in Illustrator as well as for placed objects. The Clipboard can only hold the results of one cut or copy at a time. For example, if you copy some text to the Clipboard, then at a later stage, cut an object to the Clipboard, the object you cut overwrites the previous contents of the Clipboard – the text. After you cut or copy an object to the Clipboard, you can paste it into the active Illustrator file as many times as you like.

The Copy command leaves the original on the page and places a copy of the selected object onto the Clipboard. The Cut command removes whatever is selected from the page and places it on the Clipboard.

You can use the Clipboard to cut/copy information from one Illustrator document and then paste it into another.

The contents of the Clipboard are not saved when you quit from Adobe Illustrator.

1 To cut or copy an object to the Clipboard, first select the object using the Selection tool or the Group Selection tool. Choose Edit>Cut/Copy.

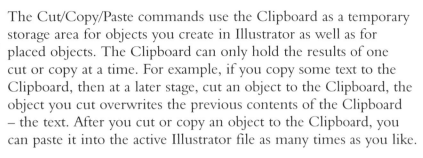

2 To paste an item from the Clipboard, make sure that you have the Selection tool selected, then choose Edit>Paste. The object is pasted into the middle of your screen display.

3 Select an object using the Selection tool or the Group Selection tool, then choose Edit>Clear to remove the object from the document completely. The Clear command does not use the Clipboard and therefore does not overwrite any existing objects already on the Clipboard.

The Pencil, Smooth and Erase Tools

There are three tools in the Pencil tool group – the Pencil tool, the Smooth tool, and the Erase tool. Use the Pencil tool to draw freeform paths, much like sketching with a pencil; the Smooth tool to create a smoother version of an existing path; and the Erase tool to erase portions of an existing path.

To draw an open path, select the Pencil tool. Position your cursor on the page. The cursor changes to the Pencil tool cursor. Click and drag to create the path. A dotted line appears on screen to represent the shape of the path.

2 Release when you finish drawing the path. The path remains selected. Illustrator automatically sets anchor points along the path to define its shape.

Drawing Closed Paths

To draw a closed path, select the Pencil tool. Position your cursor on the page. Click and drag to begin defining the path. Hold down Alt/option as you drag. A small circle appears next to the Pencil cursor. Continue dragging the cursor back to the start point. Release the mouse button, then release the Alt/option key to close the path.

Redrawing Paths

To redraw a path, select the path you want to reshape. Select the Pencil tool and position it on, or very near to, the path you want to reshape. Click and drag to redraw the path.

The Smooth and Erase Tools

The Smooth tool allows you to smooth entire paths or portions of paths, whilst retaining the overall shape of the path. The Smooth tool tends to reduce the number of anchor points in the path.

To smooth a path, select the path you want to smooth. Select the Smooth tool. Click on the path with the

If you have the Pencil tool selected, hold down Alt/option to gain temporary access to the Smooth tool.

Smooth tool to smooth the entire path. Or, click and drag along the section of the path you want to smooth. You may have to do this several times, depending on the preference settings for the tool, to achieve the effect you want.

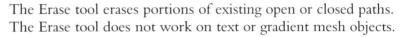

The Erase tool erases portions of existing open or closed paths. The Erase tool does not work on text or gradient mesh objects.

Paths do not have to be selected before you use the Erase and Smooth tools, just drag the tool near an existing path for the path to be affected.

To erase paths, select the Erase tool. Position your cursor on the path. The cursor changes to the Erase cursor. Click and drag along the path. Anchor points are added to the ends of any new paths that the Erase tool creates.

Setting Tool Preferences

1. To set preferences for the Pencil, Smooth and Paintbrush tools, double-click the tool in the Toolbox.

2. Enter a value for Fidelity, or drag the Fidelity slider to control how many anchor points are used to create the path and how closely the path conforms to the actual movement of the mouse. Higher values create smoother, less complex paths with fewer anchor points. Lower values result in paths that conform more closely to the movement of the mouse. These paths are more complex, with a greater number of anchor points.

3. Enter a Smoothness value, or drag the Smoothness slider to control the degree to which the path is smoothed as you draw it. Higher values create smoother paths.

The Paintbrush Tool

The Paintbrush tool can be useful when you want to quickly sketch freeform shapes, where accuracy is not too important. Before using the Paintbrush tool to create "brush strokes", you must first select a brush from the Brushes palette.

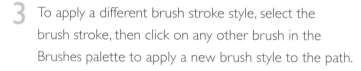

1   To draw an open brush stroke, click once on the Paintbrush tool to select it, or press B on the keyboard. Make sure the Brushes palette is showing (Window>Brushes).

2   Click on a brush in the Brushes palette to select it. A black highlight box around the brush indicates the currently selected brush. Position your cursor on the page, then click and drag to define the brush stroke.

3   To apply a different brush stroke style, select the brush stroke, then click on any other brush in the Brushes palette to apply a new brush style to the path.

Drawing Closed Brush Strokes

To draw a closed brush stroke, click and drag to begin defining the brush stroke. Hold down Alt/option as you drag. A small circle appears next to the Paintbrush cursor. Position your cursor at the start point. Release the mouse button, then release the Alt/option key to close the brush stroke path.

Applying Brush Strokes

To apply a brush style to an existing path such as a rectangle or oval, make sure that the path is selected. Click on a brush in the Brushes palette to apply the brush characteristics to the path.

The Brushes Palette

The Brushes palette contains four types of brushes – Calligraphic, Scatter, Art and Pattern. Calligraphic brushes create strokes similar to those drawn by a calligraphic pen; Scatter brushes scatter or spray copies of objects along a path; Art brushes stretch an object or group created in Illustrator along a path; Pattern brushes use a repeating tile pattern along the path. Using the Brushes Palette, you can create your own brushes, edit existing brushes and delete brushes.

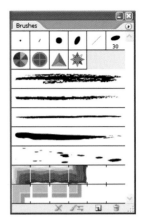

The default Brushes palette contains samples of Calligraphic and Art brushes only.

To show the Brushes palette, choose Window>Brushes.

Managing brush strokes

With a brush stroke object selected, click the Remove Brush button to revert the brushed path back to a standard path.

Choose Window> Brush Libraries, to access a range of sample brush libraries which ship with Illustrator. Click on a brush in the brush library palette to add it to the Brushes palette. The Brush Libraries sub-menu includes examples of Scatter and Pattern brushes.

2 With a brush stroke object selected, click the Options of Selected Object button. Use the dialog box to make changes to the attributes of the selected object.

3 Click the New Brush button to create a new brush. (See the next page for more information on creating new brushes.) New brushes are saved with the current file.

4 Click on a brush to select it, then click on the Wastebasket button to delete the brush from the palette. Click Yes in the warning dialog box. If you delete one of the default brushes it will reappear as a default brush in a new document after you relaunch Illustrator.

Creating a New Calligraphic Brush

You can create your own Calligraphic, Art, Scatter and Pattern brushes. The following steps show you how to create a new calligraphic brush.

1   To create a calligraphic brush, click the New Brush button at the bottom of the Brushes palette, or choose New Brush from the Brushes palette menu (⊙).

2   Select the New Calligraphic Brush radio button in the New Brush dialog box. OK the dialog box.

3   Enter a name for the new brush in the Name entry field.

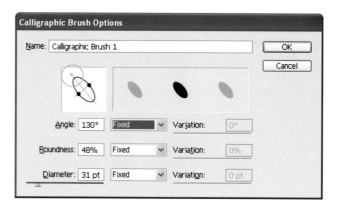

4   Either drag the arrow tip in the Brush Shape Editor to change the angle of the brush, or enter a value in the Angle entry box.

5 Either drag the black circles in the Brush Shape Editor, or enter a value in the Roundness entry box to change the Roundness of the brush.

Angle: 130°

Roundness: 48%

6 Enter a value in the Diameter field or drag the Diameter slider to specify the thickness of the brush.

Diameter: 31 pt

7 If you want to create variable brush strokes, use the pop-ups to the right of the entry fields to change from Fixed to Random. Then, enter a value in the entry field to the right of the pop-ups to specify the range of allowable variation. The brush preview box above these fields gives a visual indication of the variation values you enter.

Angle: 130°	Random	Variation: 30°
Roundness: 48%	Random	Variation: 24%
Diameter: 31 pt	Random	Variation: 5 pt

Fixed
Random
Pressure
Stylus Wheel
Tilt
Bearing
Rotation

8 Pressure is only available if you are working with a Pressure Sensitive pen.

9 OK the dialog box. The new brush appears in the Brushes palette and is saved with the current file.

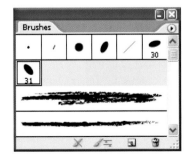

Brushes

30

31

Grid Tools

The Rectangular and Polar grid tools provide quick and flexible options for creating grids in your artwork. Both tools use the same techniques and have similar options.

The Skew sliders allow you to create grids where the spacing is varied across the extent of the grid.

1 To draw a grid select either the Rectangular Grid tool or the Polar Grid tool.

2 Set stroke color and stroke weight settings if required before you create the grid.

For a polar grid, you can select the Create Compound Path From Ellipses and the Fill Grid checkboxes to create concentric circles with an alternating fill pattern:

☑ Create Compound Path From Ellipses
☑ Fill Grid

3 Position your cursor on the page, then click and drag to define the width and height of the grid. When you release the mouse, the grid lines appear with the current stroke color and weight settings.

Polar Grid Tool Options

Default Size
Width: 1.39 in
Height: 1.39 in
[OK] [Cancel]

Concentric Dividers
Number: 5
In   Skew: 0%   Out

Radial Dividers
Number: 5
Bottom Skew: 0%   Top

☐ Create Compound Path From Ellipses
☐ Fill Grid

4 An alternative technique for creating a grid is to select the appropriate grid tool, position your cursor on the page, then click. This opens the Grid Tool Options dialog box. Use the width and height entry boxes to specify overall dimensions for the grid. For a Rectangular grid you can specify the number of Horizontal and Vertical lines. For a Polar grid you can specify the number of concentric circles and radial lines.

For a rectangular grid select the Use Outside Rectangle As Frame and the Fill Grid checkboxes to create a grid which uses the current fill color for its background:

☑ Use Outside Rectangle As Frame
☑ Fill Grid

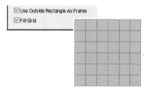

Rectangular Grid Tool Option

Default Size
Width: 2.87 in
Height: 3.93 in
[OK] [Cancel]

Horizontal Dividers
Number: 5
Bottom Skew: 0%   Top

Vertical Dividers
Number: 5
Left   Skew: 0%   Right

☐ Use Outside Rectangle As Frame
☐ Fill Grid

Flare Tool

The Flare tool creates a photographic-type lens flare effect. It consists of a combination of circular objects of varying size with bright centers, together with halo effects, rings and radial lines.

1 The Flare tool produces more interesting and usable results when you create it on top of an existing color background, as the effect depends partially on blend modes applied to components in the flare object.

To reposition the start or end point of a flare, first select the flare using the Selection tool. Next, select the Flare tool. Position your cursor on the start or end point, then drag.

2 To draw a flare and control the size and position of its main components, select the Flare tool. Position your cursor on page, then click and drag to set the start handle and define the size of the center and halo; drag in a circular direction to control the angle of the rays. Release the mouse. Move your cursor to a new position (do not click and drag), then click and drag again to add secondary rings and to set the end point handle.

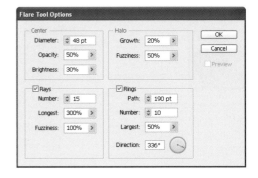

In the Flare Tool options dialog box hold down Alt/option so that the Cancel button becomes the Reset button. Click the Reset button to reset values to their initial settings, without closing the dialog box.

3 To create a flare using the Flare Tool Options dialog box, select the Flare tool, position your cursor where you want the center of the flare, then click once to display the Flare Tool Options dialog box. A flare consists of 4 main components: the center, the rays, the halo and the rings at different opacity settings. Use the controls in the dialog box to create custom settings, then click OK.

Symbolism Tools

A Symbol is an object you create in Illustrator then store in the Symbols palette. Symbols are useful when you need to use the same object multiple times in the same document. Using symbols helps keep the file size of documents as small as possible as each instance of the symbol is simply a link back to the original symbol in the Symbols palette.

Use the Symbol Sprayer tool to create a Symbol Set. A Symbol Set is a single object which contains multiple instances of a symbol. When you add an instance of a symbol to your artwork you do not increase the file size of the document as the information for the repeated symbol is stored once only in the Symbols palette.

Creating a symbol set

1 Select the symbol you want to use in the Symbols palette. Select the Symbol Sprayer tool. Click and drag to create a symbol set consisting of multiple instances of the symbol.

To create a symbol, select an object or group you want to use as a symbol. Drag the object into the Symbols palette. Or, with the object selected, choose New Symbol from the Symbol palette menu. Enter a name for the symbol, then click OK.

Symbol Shifter – moves symbols instances within the Symbol Set.

Symbol Scruncher – moves symbol instances closer together, or further apart. Click and drag to bring instances together. Hold down Alt/option, then click and drag to push instances apart.

Symbol Sizer – Click and drag to make symbol instances larger. Hold down Alt/option, then click and drag to make them smaller.

Symbol Spinner – Position your cursor over some symbol instances, then click and drag in a circular direction to rotate them.

Symbol Stainer – applies the current Fill color to symbol instances.

Symbol Styler – applies a selected Style. Select the Styler tool, then click on a style in the Styles palette. Click and drag to apply the style gradually; hold down Alt/option to remove the style.

Symbol Screener – increases or decreases transparency. Hold down Alt/option to decrease transparency.

To work with a Symbolism tool on an existing symbol set, you must make sure that you select the appropriate symbol in the Symbols palette first; otherwise the symbolism tools have no effect.

2 Double-click a symbolism tool to access the Symbolism Tool Options dialog box. Set Diameter, Intensity and Symbol Set Density for each tool. Click on the individual tool icons in the dialog box to set tool specific controls where available.

Arranging Objects

Positioning and spacing objects accurately and controlling whether objects appear in front of or behind other objects becomes critical as soon as you have more than one overlapping object in an illustration. This chapter looks at how you can change the stacking order of objects. It also looks at using the Layers and Align palettes, and at working with groups.

Covers

Chapter Four

Stacking Order

The positioning of an object in front of or behind another object is referred to as its stacking order. The order in which you create, paste or place objects in an illustration initially determines their relative stacking order.

Understanding stacking order and the various techniques for controlling it forms a fundamental aspect of working in even the simplest of Illustrator documents.

The basic principle is that the first object you create, paste or place is at the back of the stacking order. Each subsequent object you add to the illustration is placed in front of all the existing objects. The stacking order becomes apparent when objects overlap.

You can send a selected object(s) to the back of the stacking order, bring it to the front, or move it backward or forward one object at a time.

In an illustration with layers, the stacking order works on a layer by layer basis. When working on a layer the Bring to Front/Send to Back commands move an object to the front or back of that particular layer, not to the front or back of the entire illustration.

To bring an object to the front of the stacking order, select it using the Selection tool, then choose Object>Arrange>Bring To Front.

Bring to Front	Shift+Ctrl+]
Bring Forward	Ctrl+]
Send Backward	Ctrl+[
Send to Back	Shift+Ctrl+[
Send to Current Layer	

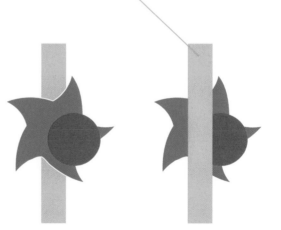

2 To move an object to the back of
   the stacking order, select it using
   the Selection tool, then choose
   Object>Arrange>Send To Back.

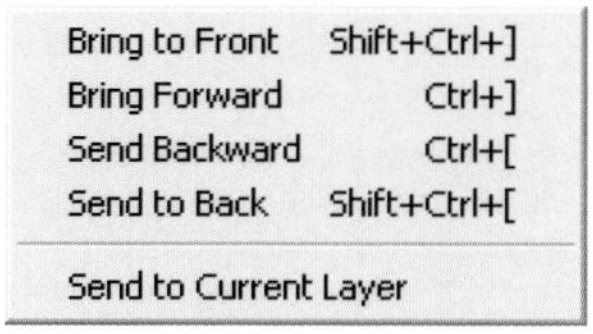

Bring to Front	Shift+Ctrl+]
Bring Forward	Ctrl+]
Send Backward	Ctrl+[
Send to Back	Shift+Ctrl+[
Send to Current Layer	

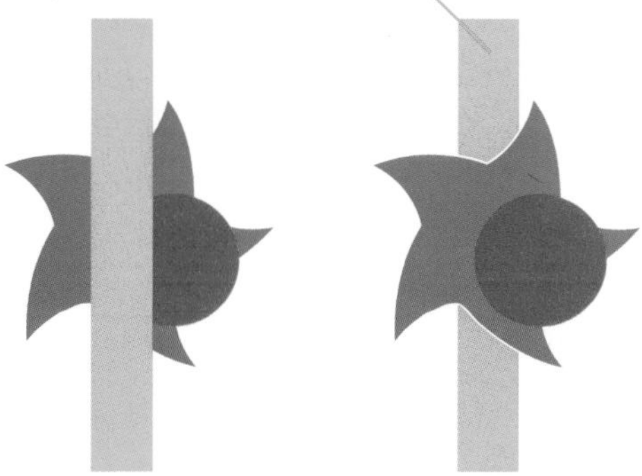

4 To move an object(s) forward or backward, use
   the Selection tool to select the object(s) you
   want to move. Choose Object>Arrange>Send
   Backward or Bring Forward.

5 To select an object that is partially or
   completely hidden behind other objects, first
   select one of the frontmost
   objects then click the right
   mouse button (Windows), or,
   hold down the control key
   then press the mouse button
   (Mac), to access the context
   sensitive menu. Choose Select
   from the context sensitive
   menu, then choose an option
   from the Select sub-menu.

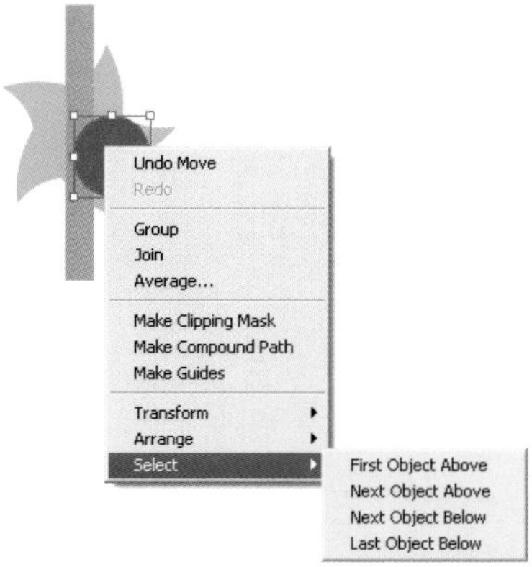

Undo Move
Redo

Group
Join
Average...

Make Clipping Mask
Make Compound Path
Make Guides

Transform   ▶
Arrange   ▶
Select   ▶   First Object Above
                     Next Object Above
                     Next Object Below
                     Last Object Below

Paste In Front/In Back

The Paste In Front/Paste In Back commands allow complete precision when changing the stacking order of objects in complex illustrations, allowing you to move an object to a precise position in the stacking order, without having to use Send Backward/Bring Forward repeatedly.

1 To Paste In Back/In Front, using the Selection tool, select the object(s) you want to paste either directly in front of, or directly behind a specific object in the illustration.

2 Choose Edit>Cut. The object(s) is cut to the clipboard.

3 Select another object behind or in front of which you want the cut object to appear. If you forget to select an object before you choose Paste In Front/ In Back the object is pasted at the back of all other objects, or in front of all other objects – the equivalent of using Send To Back or Bring To Front.

4 Choose Edit>Paste In Front/In Back as required.

Cut	Ctrl+X
Copy	Ctrl+C
Paste	Ctrl+V
Paste in Front	Ctrl+F
Paste in Back	Ctrl+B
Clear	

Hide and Lock Commands

In complex illustrations where numerous objects overlap one another, it can be very useful to hide some objects in order to work on other objects unhindered. Hidden objects cannot be selected or edited and do not print.

Lock an object so that it cannot be selected or edited. Again, this can be helpful in complex illustrations when you want to avoid accidentally selecting, moving or otherwise changing certain objects.

1 To hide objects, use the Selection tool to select the object(s) you want to hide. Choose Object>Hide>Selection. The object is hidden and cannot be selected or manipulated and does not print.

2 To show hidden objects, choose Object>Show All.

3 To Lock objects, use the Selection tool to select the object(s) you want to lock. Choose Object>Lock>Selection. Objects that are locked will still print.

4 To unlock objects, choose Object>Unlock All.

5 To lock or hide objects above a selected object in the stacking order and which overlap it, choose Object>Lock>All Artwork Above, or Object>Hide>All Artwork Above as appropriate.

Creating New Layers

Layers provide considerable flexibility in complex illustrations, such as maps and plans, providing an efficient method for managing objects. You can hide and show individual layers, lock and unlock layers, move objects between layers and specify which layers will print.

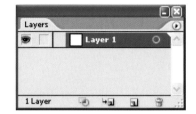

When you start a new Illustrator document you are automatically working on a layer – Layer 1. This is the default layer. For many straightforward illustrations you only need a single layer. Layers become more and more useful and necessary as illustrations become more and more complex.

Do not confuse the active layer with visible layers – many layers can be visible, but only one layer is active, indicated by the highlight and the triangle in the layers palette:

1 To create a new layer, use the palette menu button ( ) in the Layers palette. Choose New Layer.

2 In the Layer Options dialog box enter a name for the layer.

3 Choose a color from the Color pop-up menu. The color you choose is used to highlight

selected objects. This can be extremely helpful when it comes to identifying the layer on which particular objects are positioned.

4 Choose options as required. The options you choose at this stage are not permanent and can be changed at any time when you are working in the document. All the options can be changed after you have created the layer, either using icons in the Layers palette, or by selecting the layer, then choosing Options for "layer name" from the palette menu. Double-clicking a layer also takes you back into the Layer Options dialog box.

You can create sub layers within layers. To avoid confusion and over complication, it is best to use this feature only after you are fully confident with basic layer operations.

Layer Options

Show – controls whether a layer is hidden or showing when you create it. You can also use the Eye icon in the Layers palette to hide/show a layer.

Preview – leave this option selected if you want the layer to appear in Preview mode. Deselect this option and the layer appears in Artwork mode.

Lock – select Lock if you want the layer to be locked when you create it. You can also use the Lock column in the Layers palette to control the lock status of a layer.

Print – leave this option selected if you want the layer to print.

Dim – select this option for a layer if you intend to place an image (bitmap) on the layer and then manually trace around it. Dimmed images can be easier to trace around as you can see paths more clearly as you create them.

When you create an object in a document with more than one layer, the object is placed on the active layer.

5 Alternatively, click the Create New Layer button ( ) at the bottom of the Layers palette. This creates a new layer with a default name and settings. The new layer appears above the currently active layer.

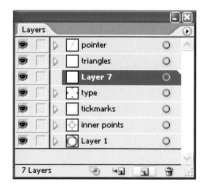

Working with Layers

When you create a new object it is automatically placed on the active layer. The active layer is the layer whose name is highlighted in the Layers palette, and which displays the white triangle (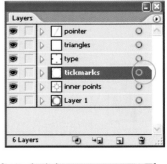) to the right of the target icon.

Only one layer can be active at any time.

1 To make a layer active, click on the layer name. The layer highlights and a white triangle icon appears to the right of the layer.

2 Click on an object with any selection tool to select the object and make the object's layer active. When you select an object on a layer, a small colored square appears to the right of the layer name. The square indicates the layer the object is on. It also indicates the color used to highlight objects on that layer. (See Step 3, page 66, for further information on setting this color.)

To select all objects on a layer, hold down Alt/ option, then click the layer name.

3 A template layer has a template objects icon, not an "eye" icon, to indicate visibility. You can still click on the icon to control visibility of the template layer. Template layers are initially locked, do not print and do not export.

4 To display a layer in Artwork mode, hold down Ctrl/Command, then click the eye icon for the layer. The eye icon changes to indicate Artwork mode. Repeat the process to bring the layer back into Preview mode.

5 To select all objects on a layer, click to the right of the Target circle. The layer becomes the active layer and the large selection indicator square appears.

Moving Objects Between Layers

As you build a complex illustration using layers there will undoubtedly be times when you need to move objects from one layer to another layer.

The relative stacking order of multiple objects is maintained when objects are moved or pasted onto a different layer. If there are already objects on the layer, objects that you move or paste into the layer are stacked in front of the existing objects.

1 To move an object to another layer, click on the object to select it. In the Layers palette the object's layer highlights. Notice also, to the right of the Target icon, a small square dot, which indicates a selected object and the active layer's selection color.

To copy an object to a new layer, hold down Alt/option as you drag the colored dot to the new layer.

2 Drag the dot to the layer onto which you want to move the object. When you release, the layer you move the object to becomes the active layer. The selection handles and the bounding box highlight around the object change to the highlight color for that layer. When you move an object to a different layer it becomes the frontmost object on that layer. You can use this technique for multiple selected objects on the same layer, or groups.

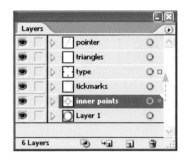

If Paste Remembers Layers is selected, when you paste objects from the clipboard they are automatically pasted back onto the layer from which they were cut, even if you have clicked on a different layer to make it active.

3 You can also use the clipboard to move an object to a different layer. First, in the Layers palette menu (⊙), make sure that the Paste Remembers Layers option is switched off (no checkmark next to it). Select the object you want to move, then choose Edit>Cut to cut the object from its current layer. In the Layers palette, click the name of the layer onto which you want to move the object. Choose Edit>Paste to paste the object into the active layer.

Managing Layers

When reordering layers, you do not have to drag the active layer, but when you release the mouse, the moved layer becomes the active layer.

Techniques for managing layers include: deleting, duplicating, changing the order of layers, hiding/showing layers, locking/unlocking layers and changing various layer options. You can also merge layers together to consolidate separate layers into a single layer and you can flatten all layers into a single layer.

1. To change the order of layers, drag the layer you want to move upward or downward in the Layers palette. As you drag, notice the thick double bar which indicates the position to which the layer will move when you release. Drag a layer upward to move

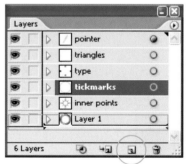

objects on that layer in front of objects on other layers. Drag a layer downward to move objects behind objects on other layers.

To select non-consecutive layers, select a layer, then hold down Ctrl/Command and click other layer names to add them to the originally selected layer.

2. To duplicate a layer, click on a layer name in the Layers palette to identify it as the layer you want to copy. Choose Duplicate Layer from the Layers palette menu.

To select consecutive layers, select the first layer, hold down Shift, then click the last layer name. All layers between the originally selected layer and the layer you Shift+click on are selected.

3. Alternatively, drag the layer you want to copy onto the Create New Layer button at the bottom of the Layers palette.

Merging layers

Select two or more layers that you want to combine into a single layer.

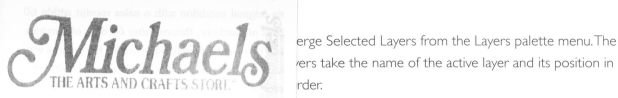
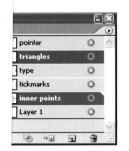

...erge Selected Layers from the Layers palette menu. The ...yers take the name of the active layer and its position in ...rder.

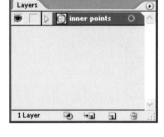

...ayers

...u flatten artwork
...le layer, make sure
...ou want included

...latten Artwork
...Layers palette menu.

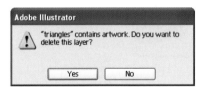

...yers

...a layer, click on
...name you want to
...hoose Delete Layers
...Layers palette menu,

...e Wastebasket icon at the bottom of the palette.

...vely, drag the layer name onto the Wastebasket icon at the bottom of the palette. Beware, no warning dialog box appears, even if there are objects on the layer, when you use this technique.

Adobe Illustrator

"triangles" contains artwork. Do you want to delete this layer?

Yes   No

Hiding and Locking Layers

The option to hide and/or lock layers becomes invaluable as illustrations become more and more complex. Both options can help you to avoid accidentally making unwanted changes to objects with which you are satisfied.

Hiding Layers

Hiding layers facilitates selecting and manipulating objects in complex illustrations in which objects are overlapped and obscured by other objects on layers higher up in the layer order.

1. To hide a visible layer, click on the eye icon for the layer. The Layer you hide does not have to be the active layer. All objects on the Layer are hidden.

2. To show a layer that is hidden, click in the now empty eye icon box next to the layer you want to show. To show all layers choose Show All Layers from the Layers palette menu (⊙).

Locking Layers

You cannot select or edit any objects on a locked layer. Lock layers when you want to avoid moving, disturbing or otherwise editing objects on the layer.

1. To lock a layer, click in the lock box of the layer you want to lock. A padlock icon appears to indicate that the layer is locked.

2. To unlock a layer, click the padlock icon. The padlock icon disappears. To unlock all layers choose Unlock All Layers from the Layers palette menu.

Working with Expanded Layers

A layer containing sub-layers, groups or objects can be expanded to show its contents. This is useful for identifying paths and whether they have appearance attributes applied to them (see page 90 for information on appearance attributes). Sub-layers and groups can be expanded in turn to show their contents.

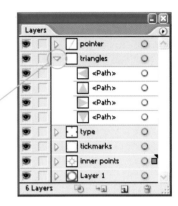

See the next page for information on using the Target icon in the Layers palette.

1 To expand a layer to view its contents, click the triangle to the left of the layer thumbnail. To collapse the layer contents, click the triangle again.

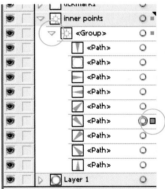

2 To expand a group, first expand the group's layer, then click the triangle to the left of the group thumbnail.

3 When working with expanded layers, click in the selection area to the right of the Target circle to select the object or group in your artwork. The large colored square that appears indicates that the object or group is selected.

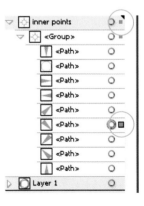

4 When a layer is expanded and you select an object in your artwork, a large, colored square appears to the right of the Target circle in the Layers palette. A small colored square appears to the right of the Target circle for the layer, indicating that there is an active selection somewhere on the layer.

Targeting Layers, Groups and Objects

When you select objects or groups in your artwork, using any selection technique, you are in effect targeting that object or group, even if the Layers palette itself is not visible.

Using the Target icon (O) in the Layers palette you can apply appearance attributes such as Graphic Styles, Effects and Transparency to entire layers, groups or individual objects. The Target icon, to the right of the Layers palette, changes depending on its status.

O = not targeted, no appearance attributes applied.

● = not targeted, appearance attributes applied.

◎ = targeted, no appearance attributes applied.

◉ = targeted, appearance attributes applied.

If you create an object on, or move or copy an object to, a layer which has appearance attributes applied to it, the object takes on the appearance attributes of that layer.

1 To target a layer, group or object, click on the Target icon (O/●). You must expand a layer to target a group or an individual object.

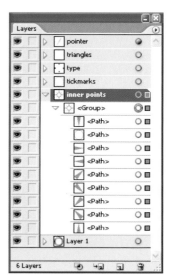

2 Either, click on a style in the Graphic Styles palette to apply the style to the targeted layer, group or object.

Basic fills and strokes do not count as appearance attributes in the Layers palette.

3 Or, choose an effect from the Effects menu to apply an effect. (See page 179.)

4 Or, use the Transparency palette to apply transparency settings. (See page 92.)

You can apply combinations of Effect, Graphic Style and Transparency attributes to a layer, group or object.

5 To delete appearance attributes from a targeted layer, group or object, drag the Target with appearance icon (●) into the Wastebasket at the bottom of the palette.

Aligning Objects

Illustrator provides flexible controls for aligning objects relative to each other using the Align palette. There are two parts to the Align palette. The top row of buttons is for horizontal and vertical alignment of objects. The bottom row of buttons allows you to space objects evenly, either vertically or horizontally, by distributing the space between them.

1. To align objects, use the Selection tool to select two or more objects. Make sure the Align palette is showing. (Window>Align.)

2. Click one of the horizontal alignment buttons to align the objects along their left edges, horizontal centers or right edges.

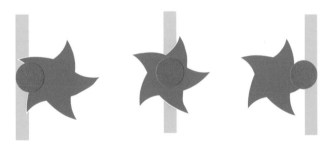

3. Click one of the vertical alignment buttons to align the objects along their top edges, vertical centers or bottom edges.

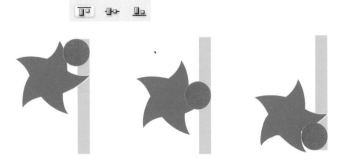

Distributing Objects

Distribute objects when you want to space objects evenly between two points. You use the bottom row of icons in the Align palette to distribute the space between specific parts of selected objects.

You must select three or more objects before you can use the distribute options.

1 To distribute objects, use the Selection tool to select three or more objects that you want to distribute.

2 Click one of the Horizontal Distribute buttons to create equal spacing between the left edges, horizontal centers or right edges of the objects.

3 Click one of the Vertical Distribute buttons to create equal spacing between the top edges, vertical centers or bottom edges of the objects.

Distributing space equally between objects

To create an exact amount of space vertically or horizontally between selected objects, enter a value in the spacing amount entry box:

Before you click the appropriate Distribute Spacing button, click one of the selected objects to designate it as the "key" object. The key object is the object around which the spacing takes effect. The key object remains static and the other selected objects move relative to it when you click a Distribute Spacing button.

1 Choose Show options from the Align palette menu, or click the palette expand/collapse button. This shows additional options at the bottom of the palette.

2 Use the Selection tool to select three or more objects.

3 Click either the Vertical button (as in this example), or the Horizontal button to create equal amounts of space between the selected objects.

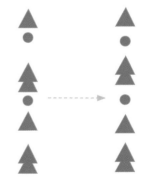

Working with Groups

If you group objects that are initially on separate layers, the objects are moved onto and grouped on the layer of the frontmost selected object.

Group objects together when you want to work with them as a single unit. You can move, scale, transform and edit groups whilst keeping the relative size and positioning of objects intact.

1 To group selected objects, select two or more objects. Choose Object>Group. A bounding box with selection handles appears around the selected shapes. Any move, scale, rotate or other transformation will now apply to the whole group.

2 Use the Selection tool to resize a group. Click on one of the objects in the group to select the group. Click and drag on a selection handle to resize all objects in the group.

Hold down Shift, then drag a resize handle to resize objects in a group in proportion.

3 To move a group, click on an object in the group to select it. Position your cursor on any object in the group, then click and drag to reposition the group. Hold down Shift, then drag an object in the group to constrain the move horizontally, vertically, or in multiples of 45 degrees. Start to drag the group, then hold down Alt/option to make a copy of the group.

The keyboard shortcut for Ungroup is Ctrl/Command+ Shift+G.

4 To ungroup, select the group using the Selection tool. Choose Object>Ungroup. The objects are ungrouped, but initially all objects remain selected. To manipulate an individual object, click on some empty space to deselect all objects, then select the object you want to edit.

The Group Selection Tool

As illustrations become more and more complex you can group one group to another group and so on to create a nested hierarchy of groups. The Group Selection tool allows you to work on objects within a set of nested groups as individual objects, or on a group by group basis, without having to ungroup the various groups.

1   To start making selections in artwork consisting of nested groups, select the Group Selection tool. Click on an object in a group. This selects one object only. If you wanted to at this stage, you could delete this individual object, or recolor it and so on.

2   Click a second time on the same object to select all other objects in the same group. It might be, for example, that you want to recolor all the objects in the group, or even delete the entire group.

3   Click a third time on the same object to select any other groups grouped with the first group. Continue to click on the same object to continue selecting outward through the grouping hierarchy.

Color and Appearance Attributes

Color can be one of the most powerful and essential ingredients of artwork you create in Adobe Illustrator. This chapter shows you how to use the Color tools in the Toolbox, how to use the Color palette to create process and spot colors and how to save, edit and manage color swatches in the Swatches palette. It also covers selecting colors from color matching systems such as PANTONE® or FOCOLTONE® color matching systems.

An appearance attribute changes the look or appearance of an object without permanently altering or changing the original object.

Covers

Chapter Five

Applying Fill Colors

When you click on either the Fill box, or the Stroke box, its icon comes to the front, indicating it is the "active" icon. If you click on a swatch in the Swatches palette, or use the Color palette to define a new color, the change is applied to the active icon.

When you create an object or path in Illustrator, it fills with the currently selected fill color and the path is stroked, or outlined, with the currently set stroke attributes. Even in the case of open paths, Illustrator fills in an imaginary line between the end points of the path. This can be disconcerting until you get used to it. Fills can be spot or process colors, a gradient, or pattern.

Use the Fill and Stroke boxes in the Toolbox to specify whether you want to apply a fill or stroke color. Use the Default colors icon to revert to Black and White as the default fill/stroke color.

See pages 85–86 for further information on working with color swatches in the Swatches palette. See page 84 for further information on creating colors in the Color palette.

1   To apply a fill color to a selected shape, click on the Fill box to make it active.

2   Click on one of the existing swatches in the Swatches palette. (Choose Window>Swatches if the Swatches palette is not showing.) The fill color is applied to the selected shape and it becomes the default color in the Fill box.

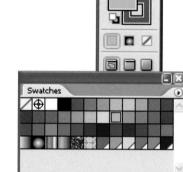

You can also apply a fill color to a selected object using the Fill pop-up menu in the Control palette running along the top of the Illustrator application window:

3   Or use the Color palette to mix a new color. (Choose Window>Color if the Color palette is not already showing.) Make sure the Fill selector icon is selected, then drag the color sliders to create a color, type color values into the CMYK entry boxes, or click in the Color Ramp along the bottom of the palette. The color you create is applied to the selected shape and it becomes the default color in the Fill box.

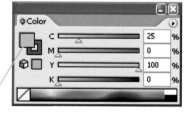

If there is nothing selected when you change the fill color, or stroke color, these settings are applied to the next shape or path you draw.

4 Alternatively, you can position your cursor in the Color box in the Color palette, or on one of the color swatches in the Swatches palette, then "drag and drop" the color into a shape. For this technique, the shape does not have to be selected. The color you drag and drop only becomes the default color in the Fill box if you drag and drop onto a selected object.

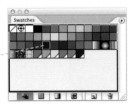

Objects with a fill of None are transparent – you can see through them to objects placed behind.

5 To apply a Fill of None to a selected shape, make sure the Fill box is selected, then click the None button. A red line through the Fill box indicates a fill of None. You can also click the None button in the Color palette or the Swatches palette.

The non web-safe warning icon appears in the Color palette if the color you create is not a web-safe color:

Click the warning color box to change the color to the nearest web-safe color.

The out of gamut warning icon appears if you create a color that cannot be recreated using process colors on a printing press. Click the warning box to move the color to the nearest printable color:

6 To apply a standard White fill and Black stroke to a selected object, click the Default colors icon below the Fill box, or press D on the keyboard.

7 Click the Swap arrows (Shift+X) when you want to swap the fill and stroke colors for a selected object.

Applying Stroke Color and Weight

A stroke is a color applied to a path. You can think of a stroke as an outline on an object. A path does not have to have a stroke; many objects you create in Illustrator will have a stroke of None.

When you apply a stroke to a path, by default, the stroke is centered on the path. For example, if you apply an 8pt stroke to a path, 4 points appear on the inside of the path, 4 points on the outside. Use the Align Path buttons in the Stroke palette if you want to align the stroke to the inside or outside of the path.

1 To apply a stroke color to a path, make sure you have a path selected. Click on the Stroke box to make it active.

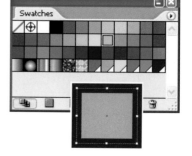

2 Click on one of the existing swatches in the Swatches palette. The color is applied to the selected path and it becomes the default color in the Stroke box.

3 Alternatively, use the Color palette to mix a new color. Click on the Stroke selector icon to make sure that it is selected (it appears in front of the Fill selector). Then drag the color sliders to create a color, or click in the Color Ramp running along the bottom of the palette. The new color is applied as a stroke to the selected path and becomes the default color in the main Stroke box in the Toolbox.

You can also apply a stroke color to a selected object using the Stroke pop-up menu in the Control palette running along the top of the Illustrator application window:

4 Another option is to position your cursor in the Color box in the Color palette, or on one of the color swatches in the Swatches palette, then drag the color onto a path. For this technique, the path does not have to be selected. The color you drag and drop only becomes the default color in the main Stroke box if you drag and drop onto a selected object.

...cont'd

You can also use the Eyedropper tool to quickly copy fill and stroke attributes from one object to another. Select an object using the Selection tool. Select the Eyedropper tool, then click on the object whose fill and stroke attributes you want to apply to the selected object.

If no object is selected when you change the Stroke weight value, the new value is applied to the next object you create.

Click the underlined word Stroke in the Control palette to apply a stroke weight to a selected path:

5 To apply a stroke of None to a selected shape, make sure the Stroke box is selected, then click the None button. A red line through the Stroke box indicates a stroke of None. You can also click the None button in the Color palette or the Swatches palette.

Applying a stroke weight to a selected path

1 Select an open or closed path.

2 Choose Window>Stroke if the Stroke palette is not already showing. By default, the Stroke palette is docked at the bottom of the Color palette.

3 Enter a value in points in the Weight entry box, or use the pop-up to choose from the preset list.

4 By default, the stroke is centered on the path. You can change the way the stroke aligns to a path using the Align Stroke buttons.

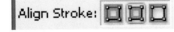

Align Stroke to Center   Align Stroke to Inside   Align Stroke to Outside

The Color Palette

Use the Color palette to create spot, process and web-safe colors which you can then save in the Swatches palette to use whenever necessary. Colors you save in the Swatches palette are saved with the document. Choose Window>Colors if the Color palette is not showing or click the Fill or Stroke box, or the Color button below the Fill and Stroke boxes, in the Toolbox.

1 To create a process or a spot color, use the Color palette menu (⊙) to choose CMYK. Click either the Fill or Stroke selector icon to make the color you create apply to the fill or stroke of a selected object.

Process colors are printed using the four process inks – cyan, magenta, yellow and black (CMYK).

2 Either drag the sliders to mix the required color, or enter values in the CMYK entry fields. You can also click anywhere in the Color Ramp at the bottom of the palette. The color is displayed in the Fill or Stroke box in the palette. If no object is selected, the color you create appears in the Fill/Stroke box in the Toolbox and the color is applied to the next object you create.

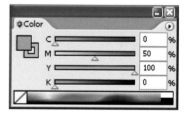

You can also drag the Fill or Stroke selector icon from the Color palette into the Swatches palette. The color appears in the Swatches palette with a default name. Double-click the default swatch name to rename the color if required.

3 To save the color, show the Swatches palette, then choose New Swatch from the Swatches palette menu. Enter a name for the color in the New Swatch dialog box. Use the Color Type pop-up to specify Spot or Process Color. The Color Mode should indicate CMYK, provided you specified this in the New Document dialog box. OK the dialog box. The color is added to the Swatches palette.

Managing and Editing Swatches

You use the Swatches palette to store colors you want to use more than once in an illustration. Think of the Swatches palette as a color library for use in a particular illustration. Customized Swatches palettes are saved with the file.

To control the appearance and content of the Swatches palette you can use a number of commands in the Swatches palette menu (⊙) together with the buttons at the bottom of the palette.

You can also use the Swatches palette to convert colors from spot to process and vice versa, to delete colors you no longer need, and to duplicate colors.

1   To control the display of swatch categories, make sure the Swatches palette is showing. Click one of the Swatch category buttons at the bottom of the palette. The Swatch palette display updates to show the swatch category you selected.

Show All Swatches   Show Pattern Swatches

Show Color Swatches   Show Gradient Swatches

2   To view swatches as a list, choose List View from the Swatches palette menu. The list view also shows icons next to each color which indicate the color mode of the color as well as whether the color is spot or process. The CMYK quarters icon indicates that the color is a process color in CMYK mode. A gray square indicates that the color is a global process color. A gray circle indicates that a color is a spot color. The Red, Green, Blue bars icon indicates that a color is an RGB color.

To select a range of consecutive swatches, click on the first swatch in the range, move your cursor to another swatch, hold down Shift and click on the swatch to identify it as the last swatch in the range. All swatches in between are selected.

Creating a new color

1 To create a new color swatch, choose New Swatch from the Swatches palette menu. Enter a name for the new color.

2 Choose either Spot or Process Color using the Color Type pop-up (see page 88 for more on global colors).

Global process colors are indicated by a small white triangle in the bottom right corner of the swatch when the palette is in Small/Large Swatch View:

3 Choose a color mode from the Color Mode pop-up. Enter values in the entry boxes, or use the sliders to create the color you want.

4 Click OK.

Editing an existing color

1 Make sure no objects are selected. Click on a color swatch to select it. Choose Swatch Options from the palette menu. Alternatively, you can double-click the swatch icon.

2 Edit settings in the Swatch Options dialog box, then click OK. Any objects to which the color has already been applied are updated depending on whether the color is global or non-global.

Spot color swatches are identified by the small white triangle with a dot, in the bottom right corner of the swatch, when the palette is in Small/Large Swatch View:

Converting a process color to spot and vice versa

1 Click on the swatch to select it, then choose Swatch options from the Swatches palette menu. Or, double-click on a swatch.

2 Use the Color Type pop-up in the Swatch Options dialog box to change the color from one type to another.

Color Matching Systems

Use the Swatch Libraries sub-menu when you want to choose a color from a color matching system such as PANTONE® or FOCOLTONE®. You can also select a color library designed specifically for illustrations intended for the World Wide Web amongst a wide range of other options.

The Web color library consists of 216 RGB colors most commonly used by Web browsers to display 8-bit images. Use this color palette to ensure consistent results on both Windows and Macintosh platforms.

To load the PANTONE color matching library, choose Window>Swatch Libraries and choose the library name from the list. The library opens as a separate palette in the Illustrator window.

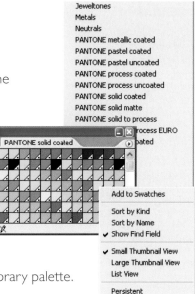

Choose Persistent from the palette menu if you want the color library palette to open automatically whenever you launch Illustrator.

Choose either Name View, Small Swatch View or Large Swatch View from the palette menu (⊙) to control the appearance of the library palette.

Selecting a color from a library

Scroll to the color you want, then click on it to select it. Or, choose Show Find Field from the library palette menu. Enter the matching system number of the color you want to select.

When you click on a color swatch in a color matching library such as Pantone or Focoltone, the color swatch is automatically added to the Swatches palette.

To add a color to the Swatches palette, drag a swatch from the library into the Swatches palette. Or, click on a color to select it, then choose Add to Swatches from the library palette menu. Any colors you add to the Swatches palette are saved with the file.

Click on a swatch in the color matching library to add it to the Swatches palette.

Global Process Colors

Global process colors are colors that automatically update throughout a document when you edit the color swatch – every object to which the color is applied updates when the swatch is modified.

Non-global colors do not automatically update throughout a document when the color swatch is edited.

A process color is non-global by default. Spot colors are global by default – you do not have the option of making them non-global.

If you create a global process color, apply it to several objects in your artwork, then edit the color, all objects to which the global color is applied automatically update to reflect the change made to the color swatch.

1. To create a global process color, choose New Swatch from the Swatches palette menu (⊙). Enter a name for the swatch.

2. Make sure the Color Type pop-up is set to Process Color.

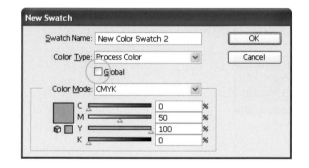

3. Select the Global checkbox to make the color a global color.

If you create a non-global process color (non-global is the default for process colors), apply the color to several objects in your artwork, then edit the color, objects to which the color is applied do not update to reflect the change to the color.

4. Adjust the CMYK sliders as necessary, or enter % values to create the color you want. OK the dialog box. The swatch is added to the Swatches palette. A global process color is indicated by a white triangle (no dot) in the bottom right corner of the swatch in Thumbnail view; a gray square in List view. In the Color palette, the representation of a global color is similar to that for a spot color.

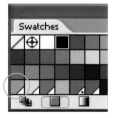

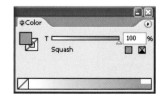

Creating Tints

Use the Color palette to create tints of spot colors, including PANTONE spot colors, and global process colors.

1. To create a tint of a spot or global process color, make sure the Swatches palette is showing. Click on an existing spot or global process color to select it.

2. Make sure the Color palette is showing. The swatch color you clicked on in the Swatches palette appears in the Fill or Stroke selector icon.

 The Spot color icon ( ), or the Global color icon ( ), appear below the Tint % entry box in the Color palette to indicate the type of color with which you are working.

3. Drag the tint slider to the left to create a tint of the base color, or enter a tint percentage in the entry box. You can also click in the Color Ramp at the bottom of the

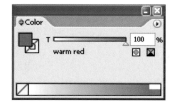

palette to choose a tint visually. Depending on which is active, the Fill or Stroke selector updates according to the value you set. The Fill/Stroke of any selected object also updates.

4. To store the tint in the Swatches palette so that you can use it repeatedly, drag the Fill or Stroke selector swatch into the Swatches palette. Or, click the New button in the Swatches palette.

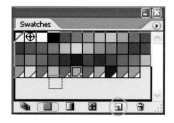

 Tints of the same base color remain related. Edits to the base color affect associated tint swatches and objects in the artwork to which the tints are applied.

5. Choose List View from the Swatches palette menu ( ) if you want to be able to identify

warm red		
warm red	50%	
Global Red		
Global Red	50%	

tints easily from their percentage value. Tints are saved with the same name as the base color, with the tint % also indicated, e.g. "Global Red 50%".

Appearance Attributes

An appearance attribute changes the way an object looks and prints, without permanently changing or transforming the original object. You apply an appearance attribute to an object, group or layer using the Appearance palette (Window>Appearance).

Fills and strokes are examples of appearance attributes – both change the appearance of the object without changing its original shape. Other appearance attributes include transparency settings and effects applied via the Effects menu. (See page 179.)

Using appearance attributes streamlines editing tasks for objects that share the same appearance (e.g. a set of website navigation buttons). The Appearance palette provides a visible and editable record of the properties of an object.

1 Notice how, as you apply fill and stroke, transparency or effects, these are recorded in the Appearance palette.

2 To edit an attribute's setting you can double-click the attribute entry in the Appearance palette. This opens the corresponding dialog box where you can make changes as required.

3 Fill and Stroke attributes can be modified independently. For example, click on the Fill attribute, then apply an effect such as ZigZag. The Effect is added to the Fill attribute as a sub attribute, without affecting the Stroke or Opacity attributes.

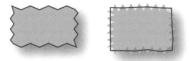

Use the Expand triangle in the Appearance palette to access appearance attributes that you have applied specifically to the fill or stroke of an object.

4 To apply an existing set of appearance attributes to an object using the Appearance palette, select an object with the attributes you want to apply. Drag the appearance icon – to the left of the Path entry – onto the target object.

5 To remove an appearance attribute from a selected object, in the Appearance palette, click on the appearance attribute you want to remove. Click the Wastebasket icon at the bottom of the palette, or drag the appearance attribute onto the Wastebasket icon.

6 To remove all appearance attributes, including Fill and Stroke, from a selected object, click the Clear Appearance button, or choose Clear Appearance from the palette menu.

7 To remove all appearance attributes except basic Fill and Stroke for a selected object, click the Reduce to Basic Appearance button, or choose the command from the palette menu.

8 You can specify that newly created objects appear with basic fill and stroke attributes only, or that they appear with all current appearance attributes applied. Click the New Art Button to toggle between the two options, or use the command in the Appearance palette menu.

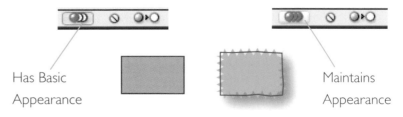

Has Basic Appearance

Maintains Appearance

Basic Transparency

To apply a transparency setting to a layer, you must first target the layer (see page 74), then enter an Opacity value or drag the Opacity slider to reduce the opacity.

You can apply transparency to any object (including text), group or layer. Underlying artwork becomes more and more visible as you decrease the opacity setting. Choose Window>Transparency to show the palette if necessary.

An opacity setting of 100% means that the object, group or layer is completely solid. An opacity setting of 0% gives a completely see-through result.

When you print or export a file with transparency settings, the transparent objects are flattened using the current settings in the Transparency panel of the Document Setup dialog box. Choose a Transparency Flattener resolution from the Preset pop-up to control the quality and printing speed of the transparent areas.

Artwork which includes any transparency effect is flattened when printed or exported. During flattening, Illustrator divides areas of transparent artwork that overlap other objects into separate components. Illustrator then determines whether to print or export these areas as vector data or as rasterized areas. This can be a complex process. Choose the High Resolution transparency flattener preset for best results.

1 To apply basic transparency to an object, first select the object. A thumbnail of the object appears in the Transparency palette.

2 In the Transparency palette, enter a value in the Opacity field, or drag the Opacity slider.

3 Transparency settings also appear in the Appearance palette as an appearance attribute.

Live Paint

The Live Paint features provide a quick and intuitive method for applying color to artwork based on the intersections of paths, rather than on an object by object basis. This can make it a much quicker technique for adding color to some types of drawings and sketches.

Before you can use the live paint feature, you must create a live paint group.

A Live Paint Group consists of "edges" and "faces". An edge is a part of a path between where it intersects with other paths. A face is an area surrounded by edges.

1   To create the live paint group, use the Selection tool to select two or more overlapping objects.

2   Choose Object>Live Paint>Make (Ctrl/ Command+Alt/option+X). A selected live paint group has distinct selection handles in order to indicate its status as a live paint group.

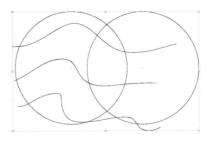

Illustrator may discard brush strokes, live effects, transparency and stroke alignment options, if objects with these attributes are selected when you create a live paint group. A warning message appears to indicate this.

3   As an alternative technique, select the Live Paint Bucket tool, position your cursor inside one of the selected objects, then click. The first click with the Live Paint Bucket tool converts the selected shapes into a live paint group. As you move the Live Paint Bucket cursor across the overlapping shapes, areas defined by intersections of existing paths highlight in red. You can use the Live Paint Bucket tool to fill these areas with color.

Select a live paint group then choose Object>Live Paint>Release to remove the live paint group. Objects that formed the live paint group become separate shapes and any live paint fills are discarded.

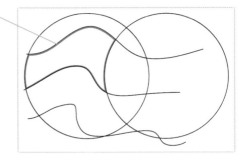

4   To fill a live paint area with color, select the live paint group, and select a fill color. Then, select the Live Paint Bucket tool and click once inside a face in the live paint group.

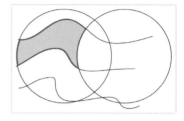

5   To apply stroke attributes to an edge, start by creating stroke color and stroke weight settings. Select the Live Paint Bucket tool, position your cursor on an edge, then hold down Shift. The cursor changes to the Paintbrush icon. Click to apply the stroke attributes to the edge.

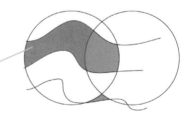

6   To delete a face in a live paint group, select it using the Live Paint Selection tool. A selected face has a dimmed highlight on it. Press the Backspace/Delete key. Other fills in the live paint group merge into the deleted face area.

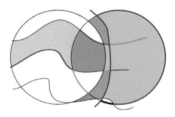

7   To add new paths to a live paint group, double-click the group with the Selection tool. A gray live paint group bounding box appears. Create a new path when the bounding box is visible to add it to the live paint group.

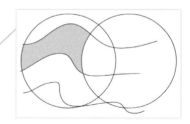

Cutting and Joining Paths

This chapter looks at a variety of techniques for cutting and joining paths, including using the Average and Join commands. The commands in the Pathfinder palette take much of the hard work out of cutting and joining paths manually and enable you to create complex shapes with ease.

Covers

Chapter Six

Scissors Tool and Divide Objects Below

The Scissors tool
Use the Scissors tool to split open or closed paths.

When you click on a closed path with the Scissors tool you create an open path. When you click on an open path you create two separate paths.

To split a path, select an object. Select the Scissors tool. Position your cursor on an anchor point, or anywhere on a curve or straight line segment, then click. The path is split at the point where you click.

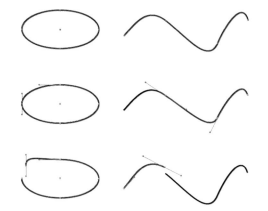

Select the Direct Selection tool, then click on either part if you want to make further changes to the shape of the path.

The Divide Objects Below command
The Divide Objects Below command works on two or more overlapping paths. The topmost path slices through any underlying paths it touches. The effect is similar to that of a pastry cutter.

The topmost, dividing object is discarded after applying the Divide Objects Below command.

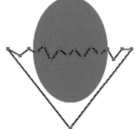

To divide objects, use the Selection tool to select the "slicing" or topmost object. Do not select the objects you want to slice.

2 Choose Object>Path>Divide Objects Below. The path of the topmost shape slices or cuts through the underlying paths. The newly sliced shapes are all initially selected. Click away to deselect, then reselect any individual shapes to which you want to make changes.

Average

The Average command aligns two or more anchor points vertically and/or horizontally.

1   To average anchor points, use the Direct Selection tool to select two or more points.

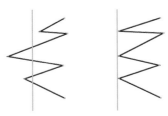

2   Choose Object>Path>Average.

3   Select Horizontal to align points along the horizontal axis:

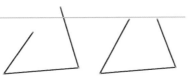

You can use the Direct Selection or the Lasso tool to create a marquee around the points you want to select, or you can Shift+click using the Direct Selection tool to add anchor points to a selection:

4   Select Vertical to align points along the Vertical axis:

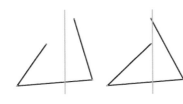

5   Select Both to align points along both horizontal and vertical axes:

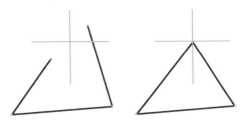

"Both" is useful when you want to join two points to form a single point. After you OK the Average dialog box, you then need to use the Join command. (See page 98.)

6   Click OK.

Join

The Join command joins the end points of two separate paths, or the two end points of an open path, with a straight line segment. If you have first used the Average command, then selected Both, so that the two points are directly one on top of another, Join simply merges the two points into one.

1   To join two separate paths, use the Direct Selection tool to select the two end points of two paths you want to join. Choose Object> Path>Join. Illustrator draws a straight line segment between the two end points.

2   To create a closed path, use the Direct Selection tool to select the two end points of the open path. Choose Object>Path>Join. Illustrator draws a straight line segment between the two end points to create a closed path.

3   To average both points then join, use the Direct Selection tool to select the two end points. Choose Object>Path>Average. Select the Both option then OK the dialog. At this stage the two end points are placed directly one on top of another.

4   Choose Object>Path>Join. Select either Smooth or Corner, according to the type of point you want to create. Click OK. The two points merge into a single anchor point.

The Knife Tool

The Knife tool is perfect when you want to cut through an object with a freeform line and end up with closed paths. The Knife tool is located with the Scissors tool group.

The Knife tool can also cut through grouped objects.

1 To cut a closed path with the Knife tool, select the tool. The object you cut through does not need to be selected.

2 Position your cursor outside the object, then click and drag across it. Make sure your cursor crosses the path to finish the cut. The result is two closed paths. The cut follows the movement of your cursor.

3 To cut with a straight line, select the Knife tool. The object you cut through does not need to be selected.

4 Position your cursor outside the object, hold down Alt/ option, then click and drag through the object. Make sure your cursor crosses the path to finish the cut. The result is two closed paths. The cut follows the movement of your cursor.

Pathfinder and Shape Modes

In early versions of Adobe Illustrator, in order to create complex shapes, you often had to use many individual objects, then cut and join paths to finally achieve the more complex path you wanted. The Shape Modes and Pathfinder commands short circuit what used to be tedious, time consuming procedures.

*Choose Window>
Pathfinder
to show the
Pathfinder palette.*

The Shape Modes

The Shape Modes group of commands typically create a new, combined or compound shape based on the overlapping areas of the original paths. The individual commands determine precisely how the resultant objects are formed.

*For further
information on
Compound paths
see page 103.*

Add to shape area – combines two or more selected objects into one merged object. Use Add to shape area when you want to create a complex outline from a series of simpler objects.

To Add shapes, select two or more overlapping shapes. Click the Add to shape area button on the Pathfinder palette. The shapes become a combined object and take on the fill and stroke attributes of the frontmost shape. You can manipulate the original shapes using the Direct Selection tool.

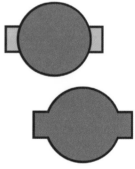

*Click the Expand
button in the
Pathfinder
palette if you no
longer want to
manipulate the original objects to
which you have applied a Shape
Modes command. You retain the
shape of the new compound
object, but discard the individual
original shapes.*

Intersect – creates a new shape where the original paths overlap. Do not select more than two objects – this command works only on two objects at a time.

To create an intersect, select two objects. Click the Intersect button in the Pathfinder palette.

Exclude – makes areas where paths overlap transparent. The result is a compound path.

| To use Exclude, select the overlapping objects. In this example the letters "d" and "o" have been converted to paths. Click the Exclude button in the Pathfinder palette. The fill and stroke attributes of the frontmost shapes are applied to the new, compound path. The white areas in this example are transparent.

The Shape Modes and Pathfinder commands work most successfully on closed paths with a fill. Using these commands on open, stroked paths sometimes gives unpredictable results.

Subtract from shape area – uses the front object(s) to cut away areas of the backmost shape where they overlap. The backmost object retains its original fill and stroke attributes.

| To use Subtract select two or more objects. Click the Subtract button.

Pathfinder Commands

In contrast to the Shape Modes commands, the Pathfinder commands create new, separate objects or paths based on where the original overlapping paths intersect.

To control whether or not unfilled objects are deleted or kept when you apply the Divide command, choose Pathfinder Options from the Pathfinder palette menu

Divide – divides selected overlapping shapes into a series of new objects based on where the original paths intersect. The new shapes created are termed faces – areas that are not divided or crossed by a line segment.

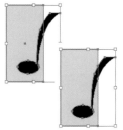

| To divide objects, select two or more overlapping objects. Click the Divide button. Choose Object>Ungroup to ungroup the resultant shapes if you want to further manipulate individual objects.

After applying most of the Pathfinder commands you can click on a shape with the Direct Selection tool, then apply a fill color if you want to apply color without ungrouping the shapes.

Minus Back – is the reverse of Subtract from shape area. In this example there are two backmost shapes – a rectangle and a circle. Objects behind the frontmost selected object cut away areas of the frontmost object where they overlap. Objects originally behind the frontmost object are deleted. The frontmost object retains its original fill and stroke attributes.

I Select two or more objects, then click the Minus Back button.

Trim – does not divide the frontmost object – this preserves its original shape and fill, but not any stroke. The frontmost object removes parts of objects behind it that it obscures. It removes strokes from the backmost shapes, but does not merge objects with the same color fill.

I To trim objects, select two or more overlapping objects. Click the Trim button.

2 Choose Object>Ungroup to ungroup the resultant shapes if you want to further manipulate individual objects.

 The Pathfinder commands do not work on Gradient Mesh objects.

Merge – removes the hidden parts of any filled objects. The Merge command is similar to Trim, it removes any strokes but it also merges overlapping objects with the same fill color.

Crop – divides underlying objects into component faces, then uses the top object to trim away all areas that fall outside its path. It also removes strokes.

 Many of the Pathfinder commands can also be applied as an Effect. (See page 179 for information on the Effects menu.)

Outline – removes all fills and divides objects into line segments only.

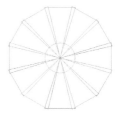

Compound Paths

You can use a compound path to create areas of transparency in objects. Compound paths handle like grouped objects, but they are not the same as a group. A compound path is one object formed from more than one path.

Compound paths formed from complex shapes, or several compound paths in the same Illustrator file, can cause printing problems. Simplify paths, or reduce the number of compounds to solve the problem.

1 To create a compound path, use the Selection tool to select two or more overlapping paths.

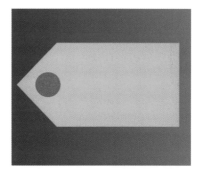

2 Choose Object> Compound Path>Make. The outer path forms the perimeter of the compound path, the inner object forms the inner boundary of the path. The area between the outer and inner path is filled with the fill and stroke attributes of the backmost object. The area inside the inner path is transparent.

| Make | Ctrl+8 |
| Release | Alt+Shift+Ctrl+8 |

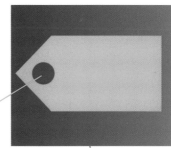

3 Use the Direct Selection tool to select and edit a specific part of the compound path – either the inner or outer path.

4 To release a compound path, select the compound using the Selection tool. Choose Object>Compound Paths>Release. The compound separates into the original objects. The frontmost object does not regain its original stroke and fill attributes.

Clipping Masks

A Clipping Mask is a path that controls the visibility of other objects. Objects, or portions of objects, that fall within the boundary of the masking path are visible. Objects or portions of objects that fall outside the path are invisible and do not print.

The object you use to create the mask can be an individual path, or a compound path. You can also use type to create a mask:

1 To create a clipping mask, create the shape you want to act as the mask on top of the objects you want to mask. In this example, the circle is the masking shape, the face and gradient rectangle underneath are the objects to be masked.

Make	⌘7
Release	⌥⌘7

2 Select the masking object and the objects you want to mask. Choose Object>Clipping Mask>Make (Ctrl/Command+7). The fill and stroke attributes of the masking shape are discarded.

3 To release a mask, select the mask object. Choose Objects>Clipping Mask>Release (Ctrl/Command+Alt/option+7). The masking shape remains unfilled with a stroke of none.

Blending Paths

The Blend tool creates a transition from one path and its fill color to another path and its fill, by creating a series of intermediate shapes and colors.

You can blend between two open paths, between two closed paths, between two gradients or two blends.

1 To create a blend between two objects, use the Selection tool to select both objects you want to blend.

2 Select the Blend tool. Click one of the anchor points on one of the paths. Position your cursor on an anchor point on the second object, then click to create the blend. Alternatively, with two objects selected, you can choose Object>Blend>Make.

Make	⌥⌘B
Release	⌥⇧⌘B
Blend Options...	
Expand	
Replace Spine	
Reverse Spine	
Reverse Front to Back	

3 Select one of the Selection tools to make further changes to the blend.

4 To release a blend, select the blend with any of the selection tools. Choose Object>Blend>Release. When you release a blend, the path or spine along which the objects blended remains as a separate object. (This is most obvious if you work in Outline mode.) Make sure you delete the path if you have no further use for it.

Controlling Blend Steps

To control the number of steps in a blend, first select the blend. Either, choose Object>Blends>Blend Options, or double-click the Blend tool.

2 Choose Specified Steps from the Spacing pop-up, then enter a value to specify

the exact number of steps you want in the blend. If you prefer, you can enter a value for Specified Distance. This value specifies the distance between steps in the blend.

Use the Blend Options Orientation buttons to specify how you want to align objects along the length of the blend. Select the Align to Page button if you want objects in the blend to align relative to the edge of the page:

Select the Align to Path button to align objects in the blend relative to the path:

3 Alternatively, choose Smooth Color from the Spacing pop-up to create a blend which has an optimum number of steps calculated to produce a smooth color transition in the blend.

Replace Spine

The spine is the path along which blend objects are arranged. After you create a blend you can use a different path as the spine for the blend.

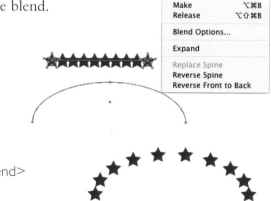

1 To apply a different path to a blend, select the blend and the path you want to use as the replacement spine. Choose Object>Blend> Replace Spine.

Creating and Editing Type

When you add text to a document, you create a text object, which can consist of a letter, a word, or multiple paragraphs. You can move, copy, delete, transform, group and paint a type object as you can for any graphic object.

Covers

Chapter Seven

Point and Rectangle Area Type T

The default Type tool can be used to create two kinds of type –
Point type and Rectangle Area type.

1 To create Point Type, select
the Type tool. The pointer
changes to an I-beam
cursor within a dotted box.
Position the cross-hair of
the I-beam where you want
to begin typing. Click to place
a flashing text insertion point. Begin typing.

Type text at the insertion point

3 When you click on
Point type with the
Selection tool, a standard bounding box with selection handles
appears. Drag handles to change the type size of the text, and also
the Horizontal/Vertical scaling.

Type text at the insertion point

4 When you click on
Point type with the
Direct Selection tool, it
is identified by a solid rectangle (the "point") and a line along the
base of the text. Drag the point or the line to reposition the text.

Type text at the insertion point

Use the default Type tool to create Rectangle Area Type when
you want to work with one or more paragraphs of text. When you
enter text into a type rectangle the text automatically wraps to fit
within the area defined by the rectangle.

1 To create Rectangle Area Type, select the
Type tool. Position the cursor at one corner
of the rectangle or column you want to
create. Click and drag to the opposite
corner to define the size of the rectangle.

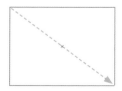

Type wraps to fit within the rectangle. Press Enter/ Return to begin a new paragraph.

2 When you release the mouse, the pointer cursor reverts to the I-beam. An insertion point appears at the start point for the text. Enter text using the keyboard.

> Start to type text into this rectangular area....|

Resizing with the Selection tool

1 Select the Selection tool. Click on the type rectangle to select it. A standard bounding box with selection handles appears, indicating the size of the area type rectangle.

> Start to type text into this rectangular area. This is type in a rectangle. The text wraps when it reaches the edge of the rectangle. When you resize the text rectangle

If you enter more text than will fit within the rectangle, a small "+" in a box appears towards the bottom right corner of the rectangle to indicate overmatter.

2 Drag a handle to change the dimensions of the type rectangle. Text inside the text rectangle wraps according to the new dimensions.

> Start to type text into this rectangular area. This is type in a rectangle. The text wraps when it reaches the edge of the rectangle. When you resize the text rectangle

Resizing with the Direct Selection tool

1 Select the Direct Selection tool. Click outside the type rectangle to deselect it. Click on an edge of the type rectangle. Make sure you do not select any of the text baselines. Drag one of the line segments to adjust the size. Start to drag a line segment, then hold down Shift as you drag, to constrain the shape to a rectangle.

> Start to type text into this rectangular area. This is type in a rectangle. The text wraps when it r the edge of the rectangle. Wher resize the text r

> Start to type text into this rectangular area. This is type in a rectangle. The text wraps when it reaches the edge of the rectangle. When you resize the text rectangle

Dragging the selection handles of Rectangle Area type does not change the size of the type inside it; it changes the dimension of the text rectangle.

2 Drag a corner anchor point to change the shape of the rectangle.

> Start to type text into this rectangular area. This is type in a rectangle. The text wraps when it reaches the edge of the rectangle. When you resize the text

Shape Area Type

Use the Area Type tool to enter text inside a path. The text is constrained by the path and wraps within it. Text can be created within any path except compound and masking paths.

1. To create text within an area or path, select the Area Type tool.

2. Position the cursor on an existing path. Click to place the insertion point, then enter text. The text wraps according to the constraints of the path.

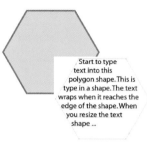

Coloring Area Type paths

When you turn a path into a text path, the path becomes unstroked and unfilled, even if it was originally stroked and filled. You can color the path, after you enter text, using the Direct Selection tool.

1. To fill or stroke an Area Type path, select the Direct Selection tool. Click outside the Area Type path to deselect it.

2. Click on the edge of the path to select only the path. If baselines appear below the lines of text you need to deselect the path and try again. Click on the Fill box or the Stroke box in the Tool palette, then apply a fill or stroke as detailed in Chapter Five, "Color and Appearance Attributes".

Coloring Shape Area Type

Just as you may want to stroke or fill an Area Type path, you often need to color the type inside the path.

1. To color Shape Area Type, select the Area Type tool. Click into the text to place the text insertion point. Highlight a range of text. Click the Fill box to make it active, then apply a color.

Type on a Path

You can have only one text object on a path.

You can enter text that follows an open or a closed path that you have already drawn.

1 To enter text along a path, select the Path Type tool. Place the cursor's baseline indicator line on the path. Click the mouse to place an insertion point on the path. Enter text. The text flows along the path.

When you create Path type, the path is reset to unstroked and unfilled. You can reapply stroke and fill attributes, if desired, by selecting the path with the Direct Selection tool.

2 To move text on a path, select the type object using the Selection or Direct Selection tool. Drag either the start or end bracket, located at the beginning or end of the text, along the path to adjust the length of the text area on the path. Drag the center bracket to reposition text along the path.

To flip text across a path, select the text object using the Selection or Direct Selection tool. Drag the center bracket across the path. Or, choose Type>Type on a Path>Type on a Path Options. Select the Flip checkbox:

3 To color the text, either highlight a specific range of text using the Type tool, or select the text using the Selection tool. Apply a fill color. To change the stroke color and/or weight, deselect the Type path, select the Direct Selection tool and click on the path. Make sure only the path is selected. Apply a stroke color/weight.

To move text across a path without flipping the type, you can use Baseline Shift from the Character palette.

4 To create additional settings for selected path type choose Type>Type on a Path>Type on a Path Options. Select an option from the Effect pop-up to control the vertical alignment of text characters as they follow a path. Use the Align to Path pop-up to specify which part of the text aligns to the path. In this example the ascenders align to the path. Use the Spacing control to create better spacing if there are problems as the text fans out along the path.

Vertical Type Tools

The Vertical Type tools create vertical text. Use the same techniques for working with the Vertical Type tools as you do for the standard Type tools.

1   To create Vertical Point type, select the Vertical Type tool. Position your cursor on the page. The cursor changes to the Vertical Type cursor. Click to set the text insertion point. Enter text. Vertical Point type does not wrap. Press Enter/Return to start a new vertical line.

See page 110 for information on coloring the type or the path.

2   To create Vertical Rectangle Area type, select the Vertical Type tool. Position your cursor on the page, then click and drag to define the size of the text rectangle. Enter text. The text aligns to the right of the text rectangle by default. Text wraps to the left when it reaches the bottom of the text rectangle.

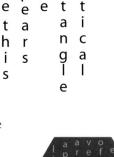

3   To create Vertical Area type, select the Vertical Area Type tool. Position your cursor on a path. (The path does not have to be selected.) The cursor changes to the Vertical Area Type cursor. Click on the path, then enter text. Any fill or stroke attributes on the shape are automatically removed.

4   To create Vertical Path type, select the Vertical Type on a Path tool. Position your cursor on a path. The cursor changes to the Vertical Path Type cursor. Click on the path, then enter text. The path is automatically unstroked.

Importing Text

You can import text prepared in other applications in a variety of common text formats which include: Plain text (ASCII), RTF (Rich Text Format), Microsoft Word 97, 98, 2000, 2002, 2003.

1   To import a text file, choose File>Place.

2   The Open dialog box appears. Use standard Windows/Macintosh dialog boxes to navigate to the relevant text file.

3   Click on the text file to select it.

4   Click the Place button. If the text file is from Microsoft Word, the Microsoft Word Options dialog box appears. Select the Remove Text Formatting checkbox to import the text as raw, unformatted text, or select checkboxes in the Include area to indicate categories of text you want to import.

5   Click OK. The text flows into your artwork, creating a default size rectangular text area. Adjust the dimensions of the rectangle using the Selection tool and apply formatting as necessary. (See Chapter 8, Formatting Type for further information on formatting text.)

Wrapping Text Around Objects

If your illustration contains text and objects that overlap, there can be times when you require the text to wrap or run around the objects, rather than appearing on top or underneath.

1 To wrap text around an object, make sure the object is in front of the text objects.

2 Select the graphic object you want text to wrap around, using the Selection tool. Choose Object>Text Wrap>Make.

3 To create a desirable text wrap effect it is often necessary to create additional space between the object and the text. To control how closely the text wraps around the object choose Object>Text Wrap>Text Wrap Options. Enter a value in the Offset entry box to specify the offset between the object and the text next to it.

Releasing text wrap

Select the graphic object to which the text wrap is applied. Choose Object>Wrap>Release.

Formatting Type

Type can often form an integral part of the artwork you create. Illustrator provides a complete set of sophisticated typographic controls that give you the precision you need to create interesting, attractive and readable type.

Covers

Chapter Eight

Highlighting Text

You can format an entire type object by selecting it with the Selection tool and then making changes to character and paragraph settings. Or, you can make changes to specific ranges of text by highlighting the text you want to format and then changing the character and paragraph settings. Use the following techniques to highlight text:

To deselect text, using the Type tool, just click anywhere within the text.

That quick, lazy, brown wolf that lopes and lunges

That quick, lazy, brown **wolf** that lopes and lunges loosely through the dusk blue orchard fragranced trees

1	To highlight text, select the Type tool. Click into a text rectangle and make sure that the text insertion point is flashing somewhere in the text. The cursor changes to the I-beam cursor.

That quick, lazy, brown wolf that lopes and lunges loosely through the dusk blue orchard fragranced trees

2 Position the I-beam cursor at the start of the text you want to highlight. Click and drag across the text. As you do so, the text reverses out or highlights to indicate exactly which characters are selected. Drag your cursor

Supply chain stretched
The research also revealed that the chemical supply chain is becoming increasingly connected and inter-related along its entire length – from 'upstream' suppliers and refiners to 'downstream' customers and end-users.
Xhead A
The implication is that chemical companies cannot achieve supply chain transformation in isolation, but need to examine and redefine the way they do business with every other participant in the chain. What is clear is that for companies that want to be leaders, the status quo is not an option.

In the chemical sector, the significance of these results is reinforced by our findings that supply chain accounts for up to 70% of companies' overall cost base, and that the difference in supply chain costs between the industry's best and average performers and another word or two was about $170m for a $3bn company.
Xhead B
Given the industry's traditional levels of return, with on-par pre-tax earnings commonly reckoned to be around $60m per $1bn for a commodity player and perhaps $90m per $1bn for a speciality player or solution provider,.

horizontally, vertically or diagonally depending on the range of text you want to select. Using this technique you must select all the text you want to highlight with one movement of the mouse. You can't release, then drag to add to the original selection. Practice this technique a number of times to get used to it. Use the technique to select any amount of visible text.

When you have a range of text highlighted, if you press any key on the keyboard you are effectively overtyping the selected text – whatever you type on the keyboard replaces the selected text. If this happens unintentionally, choose Edit> Undo immediately.

3 Position your cursor on a word, then double-click the mouse button to highlight one word.

4 Position your cursor within a paragraph, then triple-click to highlight an entire paragraph.

5 Position your cursor at the start of the text you want to highlight. Click the mouse button to place the text insertion point and to mark the start of a range of text you want to highlight. Move the cursor to the end of the text you want to highlight. It is important that you do not click and drag with the mouse at this stage, simply find the last bit of text you want to highlight. Hold down Shift, then click the mouse button to indicate the end of the text you want to highlight. All the text between the initial click and the Shift+click highlights.

You can use the same techniques for highlighting Area type, Vertical Area type, Path Type and Vertical Path type.

6 Choose Edit>Select All (Ctrl/ Command+A) to select an entire text file. This includes any overmatter, even though you cannot see it.

Font, Style, Size

Font and Style

A Font is a complete set of characters (upper case, lower case, numerals, symbols and punctuation marks) in a particular typeface, size and style. The term typeface refers to the actual design or cut of the characters. For example, Gill Sans is a typeface. There are many variations of Gill Sans within the Gill Sans typeface family.

1 To change the font for a particular range of text, make sure you select the text using the Type tool. Select a text rectangle with the Selection tool if you want to change the font for the entire text rectangle. If nothing is selected when you choose a new font you set a text default – the next time you enter text it is formatted according to the font you choose.

Character: **Myriad**

2 Either choose Type>Font and select a typeface and style from the Font sub-menus. Or use the Font pop-up and the Style pop-up in the Character palette. Choose a typeface, such as Warnock Pro, and a style, such as Semibold. You can also choose a typeface and style from the pop-up menus in the Control palette.

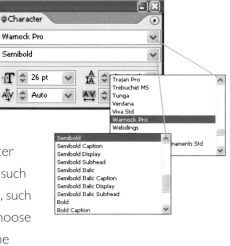

Character: Myriad   Roman   26 pt

Size

You can specify type size from 0.1–1296 points.

To specify a type size, choose Type>Size and select a size from the Size sub-menu. If you choose Other from the sub-menu the Character palette opens if it is not already showing.

2 You can also use the Size pop-up in the Character or Control palettes to choose from the preset list of sizes. Or highlight the existing value in the entry field, enter a new value, then press Enter/Return to apply the change.

26.03 pt
6 pt
7 pt
8 pt
9 pt
10 pt
11 pt
12 pt
14 pt
18 pt
21 pt
24 pt
36 pt
48 pt
60 pt

3 Or, click the up/down arrows to increase/decrease the size in single point increments. Hold down Ctrl/Command+Shift then click the Up/Down arrows to change type size in double the default increments (set in Type Preferences – see below).

4 For text highlighted with the Type tool, hold down Ctrl/Command+Shift, then use the "<" or ">" keys to decrease/increase the size in increments. The standard default for this keyboard shortcut is 2 points. If necessary, choose Edit>Preferences> Type (Windows), or Illustrator> Preferences>Type (Mac), then change the value in the Size/Leading entry field.

5 For highlighted text, hold down Ctrl/Command+Alt/option+Shift, then use the "<" or ">" keys to decrease/increase the size in increments of 5 times the default Type Size/Leading preference setting. For example, with the Type Size/Leading setting at 1 point, this keyboard shortcut will decrease/increase the size in 5 point increments.

Leading

Leading is a very important consideration for setting readable and attractive type.

Leading is the distance from one baseline of text to the next. A baseline is an imaginary line that runs along the base of text characters

That quick, lazy, brown wolf that stretches, sniffs and squeezes through the dusk blue orchard fragranced trees

Absolute Leading

Absolute leading is a fixed value. If you change the point size of your type, the leading does not change, it remains fixed. For example, if you are working with 14 point type with a leading value of 20 (14/20), then change the type size to 18, the leading value remains at 20 points.

Leading is set relative to the point size with which you are working. Typically the leading value, measured in points, will be greater than the point size. In headlines at larger point sizes, leading may need to be the same value as the size of the headline, or could even be slightly less than the headline size (negative leading).

1   To set leading for an entire text rectangle, select the text with the Selection tool. To set leading for a complete paragraph(s), use the Type tool to select the paragraph(s). To set leading for a line of type, use the Type tool and select at least one character – leading is set according to the highest leading value applied to any character in the line.

2   Highlight the Leading field in the Character palette and enter a value. Press Enter/Return to apply the value to the selected text.

3   You can also use the leading pop-up to choose from the preset list. Or use the arrows to increase/decrease leading in single point increments.

Auto Leading

Auto Leading sets leading to an additional 20% of the point size with which you are working. If you increase or decrease the point size, the leading value changes automatically.

Hold down Ctrl/ Command+Shift then click the leading arrows to increase/decrease the leading in double the default leading increments.

1   Choose Auto from the Leading pop-up. Auto Leading appears as a value in brackets.

Kerning

The kerning/ tracking unit used in Adobe Illustrator is 1/1000ᵗʰ Em.

Use kerning – often referred to as "pair kerning" – to reduce the space between two adjacent characters. Digital fonts have in-built, automatic pair kerning values. Auto Kerning is the default when you create type in Adobe Illustrator. At larger point sizes, certain combinations of character may need manual kerning; body text sizes do not normally require any manual kerning.

1 To manually kern characters, select the Type tool. Place the text insertion point between the character pair you want to kern. Make sure the Character palette is showing. Highlight the Kerning entry field, enter a value, then press Enter/Return to apply the new value.

Automatic pair kerning amounts are indicated in the Character palette by a value enclosed in brackets. Manual pair kerning amounts are not enclosed in brackets:

2 You can also use the Kerning pop-up to choose from the preset list. Choose Auto to apply the kerning value specified by the font designer and built into the font.

3 Or use the Kerning increment arrows to increase/decrease the kerning in single increments. Hold down Shift and click the increment arrows to increase/decrease the kerning value in increments of 10.

Negative values bring characters closer together, positive values move characters further apart.

4 Hold down Alt/option then use the left/right arrows to adjust kerning values. The keyboard shortcut uses the value set in the Type Preferences dialog box. The default value is 20/1000ᵗʰ Em.

WAVE
Kerning = Auto

WAVE
Kerning = 0

WAVE
Kerning = -100

To reset kerning to 0, use the keyboard shortcut Ctrl/Command+ Shift+Q.

Tracking

Tracking is used to increase or decrease the space between a range of highlighted characters and is sometimes referred to as "range kerning".

Set the Tracking preference to 5/1000ᵗʰ to kern by the equivalent amount used by the QuarkXPress tracking shortcut.

The default tracking unit used in Adobe Illustrator is 1/1000ᵗʰ Em. When you track text using the keyboard

shortcut Illustrator tracks in 20/1000ᵗʰ Em increments. Choose Edit>Preferences>Type (Windows), Illustrator>Preferences> Type (Mac), then change the Tracking amount to specify the tracking increment used by the keyboard shortcut.

To reset tracking to zero, use the keyboard shortcut Ctrl/Command+ Alt/option+Q on a range of highlighted text.

1   To track a range of text, select the Type tool, then highlight the range of text you want to track. Make sure the Character palette is showing.

2   Highlight the Tracking entry field, enter a value then press Return to apply the new value. Positive values increase the space between characters, negative values decrease it. Or you can use the Kerning pop-up to choose from the preset list.

3   Or use the Tracking increment arrows to vary the tracking in single increments. Tracking increases in 1/1000ᵗʰ Em. Hold down Shift and click the increment arrows to increase/decrease tracking values in double the default increment.

4   Hold down Alt/option then use the left/right arrows to adjust tracking values manually using the keyboard. This uses the value set in the Type Preferences dialog box.

Horizontal and Vertical Scale

Use Horizontal or Vertical Scale to expand or condense selected characters, making them fatter or thinner. Horizontal and Vertical scale can be useful for headlines and special effects. The default value for both Horizontal and Vertical scale is 100%.

Exaggerated Horizontal or Vertical Scale settings visibly distort characters, creating pronounced differences between the relative weights of vertical and horizontal strokes in the letterforms:

1. To scale type horizontally or vertically, select the range of type you want to scale using the Type tool.

2. Make sure you have the Character palette showing (Ctrl/ Command+T). Use the palette menu (▶) to choose Show Options. The palette expands to show Horizontal and Vertical Scale and Baseline Shift fields.

3. Highlight the Vertical or Horizontal entry field,

then enter a new value and press Enter/Return to apply the change. Or, use the pop-up to choose from the preset options. You can also use the increment arrows to increase/decrease the setting in 1% increments.

Use the keyboard shortcut Ctrl/ Command+ Shift+X to reset Horizontal Scale to 100% for a highlighted range of text.

CONSTANTINOPLE	**T** = 100%, **IT** = 100%
CONSTANTINOPLE	**T** = 70%,
CONSTANTINOPLE	**T** = 120%,
CONSTANTINOPLE	**IT** = 70%

4. Also, you can manually scale point type. Select the Selection tool, click on some point type then click and drag center top or bottom, center left or right handles to scale vertically or horizontally.

Baseline Shift

A "baseline" is an imaginary line that runs along the base of text characters. The Baseline Shift control enables you to move highlighted characters above or below their original baseline to create a variety of effects.

Typically, you need to baseline shift text when you place type on a path which has a visible stroke.

1 To baseline shift, use the Type tool to highlight the characters you want to baseline shift.

2 Make sure you have the Character palette showing (Ctrl/Command+T). Use the Character palette menu to choose Show Options. The palette expands to show Horizontal and Vertical Scale and Baseline Shift fields.

3 Highlight the Baseline Shift entry field, then enter a new value and press Enter/Return to apply the change. Positive values shift characters upward, negative values shift characters downward. Or, use the pop-up to choose from the preset options. You can also use the increment arrows to increase/decrease the baseline shift in 1 point increments.

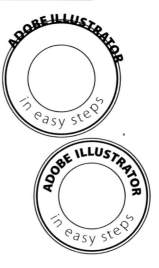

4 Or, hold down Alt/option+Shift, then use the up/down arrow keys to increase/decrease baseline shift in increments of 2 points. The increment is set in the Type Preferences dialog box. Choose Edit>Preferences>Type (Windows), or Illustrator>Preferences>Type (Mac), then enter a value in the Baseline Shift entry field to change the increment.

Paragraph Indents

Use the Paragraph palette to set indents. Left and Right indents can be set to push text inward from the left/right edge of the text rectangle. This can be useful when the text rectangle has a fill color, preventing the text from running right up to the edge of the rectangle. Indents

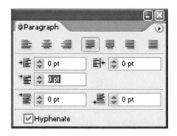

are also useful for creating bullet points. First line indents can be used to visually indicate the start of a new paragraph.

1 To set left and/or right indents, select the Type tool and highlight the paragraph(s) you want to indent. Make sure the Paragraph palette is showing.

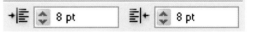

Supply chain stretched
The research also revealed that the chemical supply chain is becoming increasingly connected and inter-related along its entire length – from 'upstream' suppliers and refiners to 'downstream' customers and end-users.
Xhead A
The implication is that chemical companies cannot achieve supply chain transformation in isolation, but need to examine and redefine the way they do business with every other participant in the chain. What is clear is that for companies that want to be leaders, the status quo is not an option.

2 Enter a value in the Left/Right indent entry fields, then press Enter/Return to apply the change. Or click the increment arrows to increase/decrease the indent setting in 1 point increments.

3 To set a first line indent, select the Type tool and highlight the paragraph(s) you want to indent.

The research also revealed that the chemical supply chain is becoming increasingly connected and inter-related along its entire length – from 'upstream' suppliers and refiners to 'downstream' customers and end-users.
The implication is that chemical companies cannot achieve supply chain transformation in isolation, but need to examine and redefine the way they do business with every other participant in the chain.
What is clear is that for companies that want to be leaders, the status quo is not an option.

To set an indent using inches, enter a value followed by "in"; for millimeters, enter a value followed by "mm". When you press Enter/Return, Illustrator converts the measurement into its points equivalent.

4 Enter a value in the First-line left indent entry field, then press Enter/Return to apply the change. Or, click the increment arrows to increase/decrease the indent setting in 1 point increments.

Alignment

Alignment is a paragraph level control. If your text insertion point is flashing in a paragraph of text and you choose a different alignment option, the entire paragraph changes according to the alignment option you choose. Highlight a range of paragraphs if you want to change the alignment of more than one paragraph at a time. There are seven alignment options to choose from – Left, Right, Center and four variations of Justify.

Justify All Lines produces unsightly gaps in the last line of justified paragraphs, but can sometimes be used on headlines.

1   To change the alignment of a paragraph(s), select the Type tool, then click into a paragraph to place the text insertion point, or highlight a range of paragraphs.

2   Make sure the Paragraph palette is showing (Ctrl/Command+Alt/option+T).

3   Click one of the standard alignment buttons: Left, Center, Right.

You can also use alignment keyboard shortcuts: Ctrl/Command+Shift+L (Align Left), +R (Align Right), +C (Align Center), +J (Justify with all lines aligned left).

The implication is that chemical companies cannot achieve supply chain transformation in isolation, but need to examine and redefine the way they do business with every other participant in the chain.
What is clear is that for companies that want to be leaders, the status quo is not an option.

The implication is that chemical companies cannot achieve supply chain transformation in isolation, but need to examine and redefine the way they do business with every other participant in the chain.
What is clear is that for companies that want to be leaders, the status quo is not an option.

The implication is that chemical companies cannot achieve supply chain transformation in isolation, but need to examine and redefine the way they do business with every other participant in the chain.
What is clear is that for companies that want to be leaders, the status quo is not an option.

4   Or click one of the Justify alignment icons: Justify with last line aligned left, Justify with last line aligned center, Justify with last line aligned right, Justify all lines.

The implication is that chemical companies cannot achieve supply chain transformation in isolation, but need to examine and redefine the way they do business with every other participant in the chain.
What is clear is that for companies that want to be leaders, the status quo is not an option.

The implication is that chemical companies cannot achieve supply chain transformation in isolation, but need to examine and redefine the way they do business with every other participant in the chain.
What is clear is that for companies that want to be leaders, the status quo is not an option.

The implication is that chemical companies cannot achieve supply chain transformation in isolation, but need to examine and redefine the way they do business with every other participant in the chain.
What is clear is that for companies that want to be leaders, the status quo is not an option.

The implication is that chemical companies cannot achieve supply chain transformation in isolation, but need to examine and redefine the way they do business with every other participant in the chain.
What is clear is that for companies that want to be leaders, the status quo is not an option.

Hyphenation

Automatic hyphenation is a paragraph level control. Hyphenation is on by default. The text is hyphenated according to the settings in the Hyphenation dialog box. Switch off hyphenation if you do not want Illustrator to hyphenate words automatically at the ends of lines.

1   To switch off hyphenation, select the Type tool, then click into a paragraph to place the text insertion point, or highlight a range of paragraphs.

2   Make sure the Paragraph palette is showing (Ctrl/Command+Alt/ option+T).

3   Deselect the Hyphenate checkbox to prevent hyphenation in the selected paragraph(s).

If necessary, choose Show Options from the Paragraph palette menu, or click the Expand button (✦) in the Paragraph palette tab, to reveal the complete set of controls available in the palette.

Changing Hyphenation options

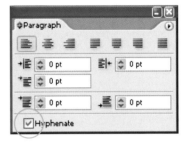

1   Choose Hyphenation from the Paragraph palette menu. Selecting or deselecting the Hyphenation checkbox in the Hyphenation dialog box is the equivalent of selecting the Hyphenate checkbox in the Paragraph palette.

2   With the Hyphenation checkbox selected, enter a value in the Words Longer Than entry box to specify the minimum number of characters required in a word before it can be hyphenated.

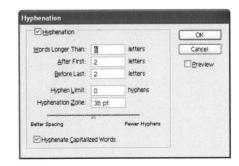

3 Enter a value, typically either 2 or 3, in the After First ... letters/ Before Last ... letters entry boxes. These settings specify the minimum number of letters that must precede a hyphen at the end of a line, and how many letters of a word must follow a hyphen at the beginning of a new line, for hyphenation to be allowed.

To insert a Discretionary Hyphen hold down Ctrl/ Command+Shift then type the hyphen key. Illustrator always breaks a word, when appropriate, at a discretionary hyphen, whether the automatic Hyphenation option is on or off.

4 Enter a value in the Hyphen Limit entry box to limit the number of consecutive hyphens allowed. A value of 2 or 3 prevents the possibility of a "step ladder" effect appearing when valid hyphenation breaks fall at the end of several consecutive lines.

5 Hyphenation Zone settings apply only when you use the Adobe Single Line Composer in left aligned text. The higher the value you set, the less hyphenation occurs, producing a more ragged right margin.

6 Drag the Hyphenation slider to control the balance between spacing and hyphens. For example, if you drag the slider towards Fewer Hyphens this can result in less attractive spacing between words and letters in justified text.

7 Deselect the Hyphenate Capitalized Words checkbox if you want to prevent words beginning with a capital letter from hyphenating.

Transforming Objects

There are five transformation tools – the Rotate, Reflect, Scale, Shear and Free Transform. You can use the tools to transform objects manually, or you can use a dialog box to transform objects numerically. You can also use the Transform and Control palettes to transform objects with numerical precision. You can transform any object you create in Adobe Illustrator. Envelope Distort, the Liquify tools and Live Trace provide further techniques to transform objects in a variety of ways.

Covers

Chapter Nine

Rotating Objects

All the Transformation tools take effect around a specific point – the reference point. The reference point marker appears at the center of a selected object as soon as you select one of the basic Transformation tools.

Rotating manually

An important point to understand when you rotate an object is that there must be a point around which it rotates. This is called the reference point.

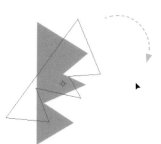

To constrain the rotation to 45 degree increments, start to rotate the object, then hold down the Shift key. Release the mouse button before you release the Shift key, otherwise the constraint effect is lost.

1   To rotate an object manually, select the object(s) you want to rotate. Click on the Rotate tool to select it. The reference point marker appears automatically at the center point of the object.

2   Place your cursor a little distance away from the reference point marker then drag in a circular direction to rotate the object around its center point.

To manually rotate a copy of the object, start to rotate the object, then hold down

Alt/option.

3   Alternatively, click anywhere on the object or elsewhere on the page to specify a new reference point around which you want to rotate the object. The reference point marker moves to where you clicked. You can also drag the reference point marker to a new position. Move the cursor to a position some distance away from the reference point marker (do not click and drag the mouse), then click and drag in a circular direction to rotate the object around the reference point.

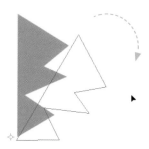

To rotate an object using the bounding box, select it using the Selection tool, then position your cursor slightly outside the bounding box. The cursor changes to the rotate cursor. Drag in a circular direction to rotate the object around its center point.

...cont'd

When you rotate multiple selected objects, they rotate as a group around a single reference point. Choose Object> Transform>Transform Each to rotate each object around its own center point.

With an object selected you can click the X: or Y: entry box label in the Control palette to access the Transform palette pop-up. Enter a value in the Rotate entry box, then press Enter/Return to apply the rotation.

If your object is filled with a pattern, make sure you select the Patterns checkbox as well as the Objects checkbox to rotate both the pattern and the object.

In the Rotate dialog box, if your object is filled with a pattern and you want to rotate the pattern and not the object, deselect the Objects checkbox and select the Patterns checkbox. The pattern rotates by the specified amount.

The Rotate dialog box

The Rotate dialog box is useful when you need to rotate an object by a precise amount.

1 To rotate using the Rotate dialog box, select the object(s) you want to rotate.

2 Double-click the Rotate tool, or choose Object>Transform>Rotate. Notice the reference point marker which appears at the center of the object. This marks the point around which the transformation takes place.

3 Enter a value from -360 to 360. Negative numbers rotate an object in a clockwise direction; positive numbers rotate in a counterclockwise direction.

4 Click the Preview option if you want to see a preview of the rotation before you OK the dialog box. Click OK to rotate the object around its center point.

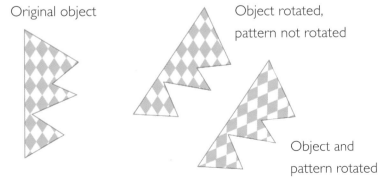

Original object

Object rotated, pattern not rotated

Object and pattern rotated

Scaling Objects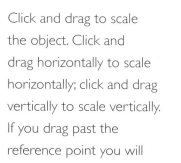

Hold down Shift, then click and drag to scale in proportion.

You can scale objects manually using the Scale tool, or using the Scale dialog box. As with all transformations, scaling takes place around the reference point marker.

1 To scale an object manually, select the object(s) you want to scale. Select the Scale tool. The reference point marker (✧) appears automatically at the center point of the object. Position your cursor some distance away from the reference point marker.

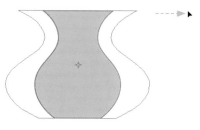

The further away from the reference point that you position the cursor before you start to scale, the greater the control you have over the transformation.

2 Click and drag to scale the object. Click and drag horizontally to scale horizontally; click and drag vertically to scale vertically. If you drag past the reference point you will "flip" the object horizontally and/or vertically.

3 Alternatively, click on the object or elsewhere on the page to specify a new reference point around which you want to scale the object. The reference point marker moves to where you clicked. You can also drag the reference point marker to a new position.

To make a copy of the object as you scale, start to scale the object, then hold down Alt/option.

4 Move the arrowhead cursor to a position some distance away from the reference point marker (do not click and drag), then click and drag to scale the object.

The Scale dialog box

The Scale dialog box is useful when you need to scale an object by a precise amount.

If your object is filled with a pattern, select the Patterns checkbox to scale the pattern as well as the object:

1   To scale using the Scale dialog box, select the object(s) you want to scale.

2   Either, double-click the Scale tool, or choose Object>Transform>Scale. Notice the reference point marker which appears at the center of the object, setting the point around which the transformation takes place.

3   Click the Uniform button to maintain the proportions of the object as you scale. Click the Non-Uniform button to scale the object non-proportionally. Enter the scale values you require.

If your object is filled with a pattern and you want to scale the pattern and not the object, deselect the Objects checkbox and select the Pattern checkbox. The pattern will scale by the specified amount.

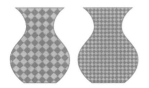

Scale
⦿ Uniform
Scale: `100` %
○ Non-Uniform
Horizontal: `100` %
Vertical: `100` %
Options
☐ Scale Strokes & Effects
☑ Objects   ☑ Patterns
OK
Cancel
Copy
☐ Preview

4   Click the Preview option if you want to see a preview of the scale before you OK the dialog box to scale the object around its center point.

5   Click the Copy button to create a scaled copy of the original object.

Scaling Stroke Weight and Effects

When you scale an object, any stroke weight is not scaled by default. For example, if you scale a circle with a 6pt stroke to 50% of its original size, the smaller circle still has a 6 point stroke.

1 To scale an object and its stroke weight, and any effects applied using the Effects menu,
first select the object(s).
Either double-click the
Scale tool, or choose
Object>Transform>Scale.

2 Select the Scale Strokes and Effects option. Now if you scale an object with a 6 point stroke to 50%, the stroke weight scales to 3 points.

3 If you want stroke weight and any effects applied using the Effects menu to scale along with an object by default, choose Edit>Preferences>General (Windows), or Illustrator> Preferences>General (Mac), then select the Scale Strokes and Effects checkbox.

Scale Stroke and
Effects selected

Scale Stroke and
Effects selected

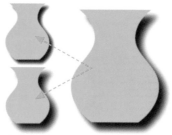

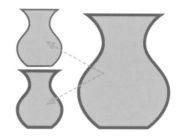

Scale Stroke and
Effects not selected

Scale Stroke and
Effects not selected

Reflecting Objects

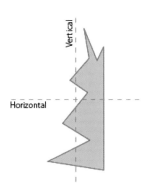

Reflecting shapes is useful when you need to create a mirrored version of your object and is an essential technique for creating perfectly symmetrical shapes. You can reflect objects manually using the Reflect tool, or using the Reflect dialog box.

1 To reflect an object manually, select the object(s) you want to reflect. Select the Reflect tool. The reference point marker (✧) appears automatically at the center point of the object.

Hold down Shift, then click and drag to constrain the reflection to multiples of 45 degrees.

2 Position your cursor some distance above the reference point marker, then click and drag upward to reflect the object across its vertical axis.

3 Position your cursor some distance to the right or left of the reference point marker, then click and drag horizontally to reflect the object across its horizontal axis.

To make a copy of the object as you reflect, start to reflect the object, then hold down Alt/option.

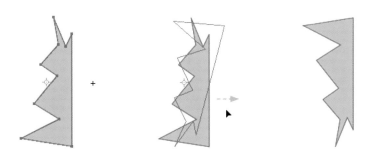

...cont'd

If your object is filled with a pattern, select the Patterns option to reflect the pattern as well as the object.

4 Alternatively, click on the object or elsewhere on the page to specify a new reference point around which you want to reflect the object. The reference point marker moves to where you clicked. You can also drag the reference point marker to a new position.

5 Move the arrowhead cursor to a position some distance away from the reference point marker (do not click and drag), then click and drag to reflect the object.

The Reflect dialog box
The Reflect dialog box is especially useful for reflecting an object precisely across either the horizontal or vertical axis.

To reflect the pattern and not the object, deselect the Objects checkbox and select the Patterns checkbox.

1 To reflect using the Reflect dialog box, select the object(s) you want to reflect. Either double-click the Reflect tool, or choose Object> Transform>Reflect. The reference point marker appears at the center of the object.

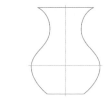

2 Click the Horizontal button to create a horizontal reflection, click the Vertical button to create a vertical reflection.

3 Click the Copy button to reflect a copy of the original object. This can be useful if you want to create a symmetrical shape. Use the Join command on the open end points of the two shapes to create a closed path. (See page 98 for information on using the Join command.)

Shearing Objects

Shearing an object slants the object along its horizontal or vertical axis. Shear is useful for creating shadow-like effects.

You get good control over the Shear operation if you move your cursor away from the reference point at an angle of 45 degrees, before you start to click and drag to perform the shear.

1 To Shear an object manually, select the object(s) you want to shear. Select the Shear tool. The reference point marker (✧) appears automatically at the center point of the object.

2 Position your cursor some distance to the right or left of the reference point marker, then click and drag horizontally to shear the object across its horizontal axis.

Hold down Shift, then click and drag to constrain the shear to multiples of 45 degrees.

3 Position your cursor some distance above the reference point marker, then click and drag upward to shear the object across its vertical axis.

4 Alternatively, click on the object or elsewhere on the page to specify a new reference point around which you want to shear the object. The reference point marker moves to where you clicked. You can also drag the reference point marker to a new position.

To make a copy of the object as you shear, start to shear the object, then hold down Alt/option.

5 Move the arrowhead cursor to a position some distance away from the reference point marker (do not click and drag), then click and drag to shear the object.

If your object is filled with a pattern, select the Patterns checkbox to shear the pattern as well as the object.

The Shear dialog box

The Shear dialog box is especially useful for shearing an object precisely along either the horizontal or vertical axis.

1   To shear using the Shear dialog box, select the object(s) you want to shear. Either double-click the Shear tool, or choose Object> Transform>Shear. The reference point marker appears at the center of the object.

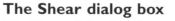

Shear

Shear Angle: 27.823 °

Axis
○ Horizontal
○ Vertical
● Angle: 0 °

Options
☑ Objects   ☑ Patterns

OK
Cancel
Copy
☑ Preview

To shear a pattern and not the object, deselect the Objects checkbox and select the Patterns checkbox.

2   Enter a value for the Shear angle, then click the Horizontal button to create a horizontal shear; click the Vertical button to create a vertical shear.

3   Click the Preview option if you want to see a preview of the shear before you OK the dialog box.

4   Click the Copy button to create a sheared copy of the original object.

The Free Transform Tool

The Free Transform tool is a convenient and powerful multi-purpose tool for transforming and distorting objects.

Rotating objects

1 To rotate an object, use the Selection tool to select the object. Select the Free Transform tool.

 As you rotate an object, hold down Shift to constrain the transformation to multiples of 45 degrees.

2 Position your cursor just outside the bounding box of the object(s). The cursor changes to a bidirectional, curved arrow. Click and drag in a circular direction.

Reflecting an object

1 Use the Selection tool to select the object. Select the Free Transform tool.

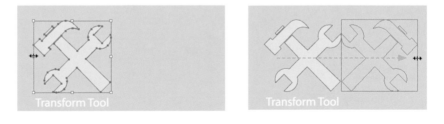

 2 Position your cursor on a selection handle, then drag the handle completely across the opposite handle or edge.

Hold down Shift, then drag a corner handle to maintain the proportions of the object as you scale.

Scaling an object

Use the Selection tool to select the object. Select the Free Transform tool. Drag a selection handle on the bounding box.

Hold down Alt/option and drag a selection handle to scale from the center of the object.

Shearing an object

Use the Selection tool to select the object. Select the Free Transform tool.

2   Position your cursor on a side handle (center top or bottom, center left or right, but not a corner handle). Start to drag the handle, then hold down Ctrl/Command+Alt/option as you drag.

Distorting an object

Use the Selection tool to select the object. Select the Free Transform tool.

2   Position your cursor on a corner handle, start to drag, then hold down Ctrl/Command.

3   To create a perspective effect, position your cursor on a corner handle, start to drag, then hold down Ctrl/Command+ Alt/option+Shift.

The Transform and Control Palettes

To access the pop-up Transform palette controls from the Control palette, click the X: or Y: entry box label in the Control palette.

You can use the Transform or Control palettes to position, scale, rotate and shear objects. To show the Transform palette, choose Window>Transform. The Control palette displays along the top of the Illustrator screen, below the menu bar, by default. If it is not visible, choose Window>Control Palette.

Both palettes allow you to choose a reference point on a selected object which becomes the reference point for the changes you make.

1 To choose a reference point, click one of the reference point handles in the palette. These reference point handles refer to the corresponding selection handles on the bounding box of the selected object. The selected reference point appears solid.

Options in the Transform palette menu allow you to reflect objects, scale stroke weights and specify whether or not pattern fills are transformed.

2 To reposition an object, enter values in the X and/or Y entry fields. The X value positions the reference point from the left edge of the page; the Y value positions the object from the bottom of the page. Press Enter/Return to apply the change.

The default position for the zero point is the bottom left corner of the artboard. To reset the zero point, make sure the rulers are showing, then double-click in the corner box where the left and top rulers meet.

3 To scale an object, enter values in the W and H fields to scale the object to that size. Click the chain icon before you enter either a width or height value to scale the object in proportion.

4 To rotate an object, enter a value in the Rotate entry field, or use the pop-up to choose from the preset list. To Shear an object, enter a value in the Shear entry field, or use the pop-up to choose from the preset list.

Envelope Distort

The Envelope Distort sub-menu provides a range of powerful options for distorting Illustrator objects and groups. There are three methods to choose from: Make with Warp, Make with Mesh and Make with Top Object.

Make with Warp

Select the Preview checkbox in the Warp Options dialog box to see a preview of how settings you create affect the selected objects.

1 Select an object or group using the Selection tool. Choose Envelope>Distort>Make with Warp.

2 In the Warp Options dialog box, choose a preset from the Style pop-up menu to set the basic shape for the warp effect.

3 Drag the Bend slider to control the extent and direction of the warp, or enter a value from -100 to 100% in the Bend entry box.

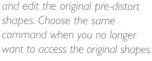

After you apply an envelope distort effect you can choose Object>Envelope Distort>Edit Contents to access and edit the original pre-distort shapes. Choose the same command when you no longer want to access the original shapes.

4 Use the Horizontal and Vertical Distortion controls to apply further directional distortion to the warp.

Make with Mesh

For a selected object or group, choose Object>Envelope Distort>Make with Mesh.

Choose Object>Envelope Distort>Expand to permanently change the original objects into their new distorted shape.

2 In the Envelope Mesh dialog box enter Row and Column values to define the initial mesh grid. Click OK to create the Mesh.

3 A mesh distort envelope is similar in concept to a gradient mesh object. Use the Direct Selection tool to edit the mesh distort grid. (See page 166 for information on editing mesh points.)

Make with Top Object

If you no longer want to distort an object using an envelope, choose Object>Envelope Distort>Release. Release returns the original shapes to their initial state and also creates a separate envelope shape.

1 Create an object you want to use as the distort envelope and position it on top of the object you want to distort.

2 Select both objects, then choose Object>Envelope Distort>Make with Top Object.

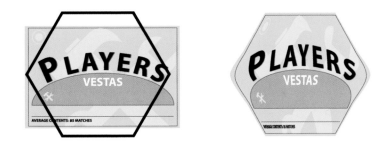

3 Use the Direct Selection tool to edit the path of the top object if required.

Liquify Tools

Use the Liquify tools to rapidly transform and distort objects in a variety of interesting ways.

You cannot use the Liquify tools on text, graphs or symbols.

To liquify an object, select one of the Liquify tools then position your cursor on the object. You can keep the mouse static as you press the mouse button to apply the effect, or you can click and drag.

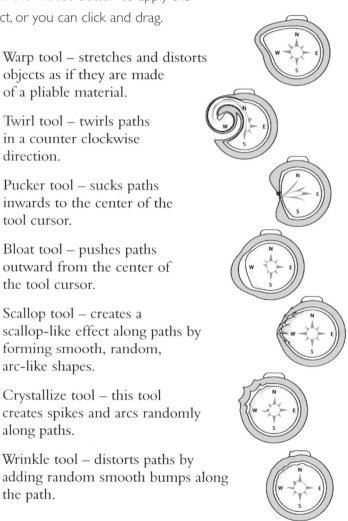

 Warp tool – stretches and distorts objects as if they are made of a pliable material.

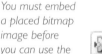 Twirl tool – twirls paths in a counter clockwise direction.

 Pucker tool – sucks paths inwards to the center of the tool cursor.

You must embed a placed bitmap image before you can use the Liquify tools to modify it. To embed a placed image, choose Embed from the Links palette menu.

Bloat tool – pushes paths outward from the center of the tool cursor.

Scallop tool – creates a scallop-like effect along paths by forming smooth, random, arc-like shapes.

Crystallize tool – this tool creates spikes and arcs randomly along paths.

Double-click a Liquify tool to access the tool's Options dialog box. You can control Width, Height, Angle and Intensity settings for all tools, as well as tool specific options for each individual effect.

Wrinkle tool – distorts paths by adding random smooth bumps along the path.

Live Trace

The Live Trace command allows you to quickly transform a bitmap image into vector artwork. You can control the number of objects the live trace command creates, as well as the complexity, accuracy and detail in the resultant paths.

1 Place a bitmap image into your Illustrator document. (See page 38 for information on placing files.)

The Live trace preset you choose will depend on the type of bitmap image you have on screen and the kind of result you want to achieve. The screen shots in this example use the Color 16 preset.

2 Make sure the image remains selected. Click on the Tracing Presets and Options button to the right of the Live Trace button in the Control palette, then select one of the presets. Depending on the speed of your computer and the complexity of the preset trace requirements, the results of the trace are visible on screen within a few seconds.

Live Trace provides real flexibility for creating exactly the results you want as you can continue to edit settings until you are satisfied. You can then Expand the trace to work with the resulting vector shapes if required.

3 At this stage the trace remains "live" – you can adjust any of the trace settings to alter and fine tune the results. In the Tracing Control palette, use the Preset pop-up menu to choose a different preset, or click the Tracing Options button to access the Tracing Options dialog box. The Tracing Options dialog box provides a complete set of detailed controls for tracing objects.

You can use the Preview Image and Preview Tracing pop-up menus to control the on-screen appearance of the trace object. This can help you to evaluate the results of the trace. For example, choose No Tracing Result from the Preview Trace pop-up and Original Image from the Preview Image pop-up to hide the trace results and show only the original bitmap image.

4 With a live trace object selected the Control palette changes to provide options for controlling the trace results. Use the Max Colors entry box to specify how many colors you want in the traced object. The higher the number the greater the amount of detail and complexity in the resulting vector shapes.

Lower values tend to produce fewer, simpler shapes. Min Area specifies the smallest area of detail to be traced.

Converting a traced object

When you are satisfied with the results of the Live Trace you can convert it into vector artwork which you can then continue to manipulate, or you can convert it into a Live Paint object which you can fill with color.

To set the default tracing preset, choose Object>Live Trace>Tracing Options. Choose an option from the Presets pop-up menu, then click the Set Default button. When you click the Live Trace button to trace a bitmap, Illustrator uses this as its default setting to perform the initial trace operation.

1 Make sure the Live Trace object is selected. Click the Expand button in the Control palette, or choose Object>Live Trace>Expand. Illustrator creates vector shapes according to the trace settings.

2 The vector shapes are initially grouped. Choose Object>Ungroup, click on some empty space to deselect all the previously grouped objects, then click on an individual shape to manipulate it further. Alternatively, you can use the Direct Selection tool to manipulate individual shapes without ungrouping.

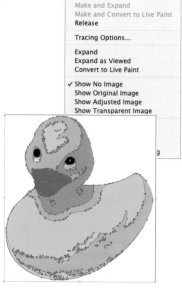

To discard the tracing object, but retain the original placed image, choose Object>Live Trace>Release.

Bezier Paths and the Pen Tool

Bezier curves are the fundamental building blocks of all objects you create in Adobe Illustrator. An understanding of Bezier curves is essential for working efficiently in Illustrator and if you want to unlock the full creative possibilities of the application. The ideas and techniques associated with working with Bezier curves can take a little while to master, but it is well worth spending the time to do so.

Covers

Chapter Ten

Bezier Paths

Paths form the skeleton of all the shapes you create in Adobe Illustrator. You can edit anchor points, curve and line segments and you can also adjust direction points which control the shape and length of curve segments.

Points and Line Segments

A path consists of two or more anchor points joined by curve or straight line segments.

Open Paths

Create open paths using the Pen, Pencil and Brush tools and the Spiral tool. The start and end points of an open path do not join up.

Closed Paths

Create closed paths using tools such as the Oval, Rectangle, Star, and Polygon tools. These tools automatically create a closed path. You can also create closed paths using the Brush and Pencil tools (see Chapter Three) and the Pen tool (see page 149).

You can apply a fill and/or stroke to an open or closed path. (See Chapter Five, Color and Appearance Attributes.)

Anchor points

Illustrator sets anchor points automatically when you create most paths. Using the Pen tool you can control exactly where anchor points are created and which type of anchor point you create. Anchor points help define the exact shape of the path. You can edit anchor points to change the shape of the path.

You must use the Direct Selection tool to edit the anchor points which form a path.

Direction points and lines

Anchor points connecting curve segments have associated direction points, joined to the anchor point by a direction line. Direction points control two aspects of the curve – its length and direction. The direction points associated with an anchor point become visible when you click on the anchor point with the Direct Selection tool.

The Pen Tool

Use the Pen tool to create open or closed paths. Using the Pen tool gives you complete control over where you position each anchor point and the type of anchor point you create. You can use the Pen tool to create straight line segments, curve segments, or a mixture of both.

1 To create a straight line segment, select the Pen tool. Position your cursor on the page, then click. This sets the first anchor point. Move the cursor to a new position (do not click and drag), and then click. This sets the next anchor point and a line segment is drawn between the anchor points. Continue the procedure to create as many straight line segments as you need.

2 To finish drawing the path, either position your cursor back at the start point (a small circle appears with the cursor), then click to create a closed path. Or, click on the Pen tool (or any other tool) in the Toolbox to create an open path. You can also choose Edit>Deselect All to create an open path.

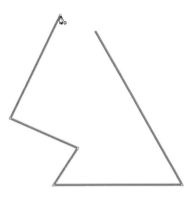

To make adjustments to a path as you draw it, hold down Ctrl/Command to temporarily access the Direct Selection tool. Make adjustments, then release the Ctrl/Command key to continue drawing the path with the Pen tool.

3 To create curve segments, select the Pen tool. Position your cursor on the page, then click and drag. This action sets the first anchor point and defines its associated direction points.

You can use both the straight and curve segment techniques to create paths consisting of curve and straight line segments.

Release the mouse. Move the cursor to a new position. Click and drag to set another anchor point and to define the associated direction points. Continue the procedure to create as many curve segments as you require.

To add straight line or curve segments to an existing path, select an end point using the Direct Selection tool, then select the Pen tool. Click on the end point, or click and drag on the end point, move your cursor to a new position, then continue to click and drag or click to add to the path.

4 To finish drawing the path, either position your cursor back at the start point (a small circle appears with the cursor), then click to create a closed path. Or, click on the Pen tool (or any other tool) in the Toolbox to create an open path. You can also choose Edit>Deselect All to create an open path.

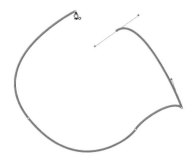

Add and Delete Anchor Points

You can add and delete anchor points using the Add Anchor Point and Delete Anchor Point tools respectively.

You can add and delete points on all basic shapes such as ovals, rectangles, and stars.

1 To add an anchor point to a path, select the Add Anchor Point tool. Position your cursor on the path (the path does not have to be selected), then click to add a point. Points added on a curve segment automatically appear with direction points. Points added to straight line segments do not have direction points.

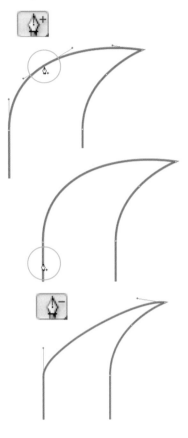

2 To delete anchor points, make sure the path is selected. Select the Delete Anchor Point tool. Position your cursor on an existing anchor point, then click to delete the point. The path redraws without the point.

The more points there are in an illustration, the more complex it becomes and the longer it takes to print. It is always a good idea to work with as few points as necessary to achieve the shapes you require. This helps to ensure trouble-free output.

Using the Pen tool to add and delete points

1 Select a path, using one of the selection tools. Select the Pen tool. Position your cursor on a curve or straight line segment. The cursor changes to the Add Anchor Point cursor. Click to add an anchor point.

2 Alternatively, position your cursor on an existing anchor point. The cursor changes to the Delete Anchor Point cursor. Click to delete the anchor point. The path redraws accordingly.

Selecting Anchor Points

You typically need to edit paths to achieve the exact path you want. To do this you must select and manipulate anchor points and direction points. Use the Direct Selection tool to select and manipulate points.

1   To select anchor points, select the Direct Selection tool. If the path you want to edit is already selected, click away from the object to deselect the shape. Click back on the path. The path is selected and anchor points should appear as hollow squares. If you click on a curve segment, direction lines may also appear. (If you use the Direct Selection tool and click in the fill area of a filled path you select the object as if you are using the Selection tool. This means you cannot click on individual anchor points to select them.)

2   Click on an anchor point to select it. If the anchor point has associated direction points they appear when you select the anchor point. A selected point is represented by a solid square.

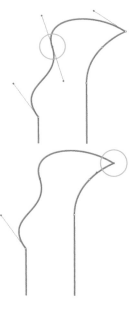

3   To select more than one anchor point, select the first point, then hold down Shift and click on the other points you want to add to the selection. Direction points disappear when you select more than one anchor point.

You can create a more freeform, irregular selection of points using the Lasso tool.
Click and drag around the points you want to select. Points included in the marquee area are selected when you release the mouse button:

4   You can use the Direct Selection tool to marquee-select multiple points. Position the Direct Selection tool cursor outside the path, then click and drag to define the selection marquee (dotted rectangle).

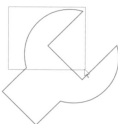

Editing Anchor Points and Segments

Once you have selected the anchor point(s) you want to work on, you can then make changes to the shape of a path by repositioning them. You edit anchor points using the Direct Selection tool.

If all the anchor points are solid, dragging an anchor point moves the entire path, not individual points. If this happens, click away from the object to deselect it, then click back on the path (not the fill).

1   To edit anchor points, first select the anchor point(s) you want to work on. Still using the Direct Selection tool, position your cursor on the point then click and drag to reposition the point(s). The path redraws accordingly.

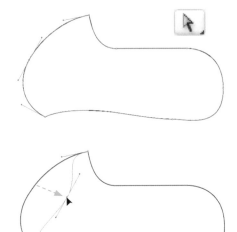

2   Start to drag the point, then hold down the Shift key to constrain the movement of the point(s) vertically, horizontally or at increments of 45 degrees.

3   Or, with the point(s) selected, press the arrow keys on the keyboard to nudge the points in 1 point increments.

4   Alternatively, position your cursor on a curve or straight line segment, then click and drag to edit the shape of the path. Be very careful as you use this technique as you can easily produce major distortions of the path with relatively small movements of the cursor.

Using the Reshape Tool

The Reshape tool enables you to select sections of a path consisting of more than one anchor point and adjust them globally, maintaining the overall shape of the path.

1   To adjust a path using the Reshape Tool, use the Direct Selection or Lasso tool to select the points you want to edit.

2   Select the Reshape tool. Position your cursor on one of the selected points, then click. This becomes the focal point for the changes you make.

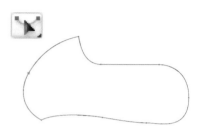

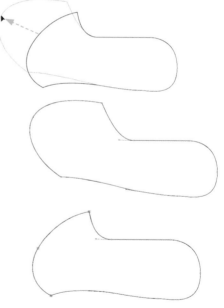

3   Drag the focal point to adjust the path, maintaining the overall shape for the selected portion of the path.

4   You can hold down Shift, then click on additional points if you want to create several focal points for the reshape operation.

5   If you click on a curve or straight line segment with the Reshape tool, a new anchor point is added to the path.

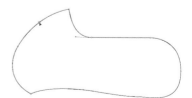

Editing Direction Points

When you click on an anchor point with a curve segment entering or leaving the point, you also see one or two direction points associated with the anchor point. These direction points control the length and shape of the curve segments.

Use the Direct Selection tool to edit direction points.

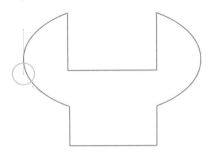

1 To edit direction points, first select the curve point on which you want to work. When you click on an anchor point on a curve, direction points appear. Direction points control the length and shape of a curve segment.

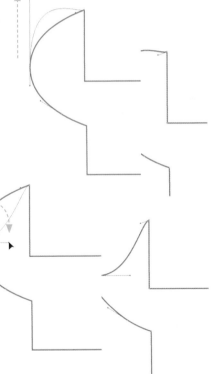

2 Drag a direction point further away from the anchor point to increase the length of the curve segment. Drag the direction point closer to the anchor point to make the curve segment shorter.

3 Drag a direction point in a circular direction to change the angle at which the curve leaves or enters the point. This changes the shape of the curve segment.

Smooth and Corner Points

Use the Direct Selection tool to edit anchor points and direction points.

It is important to be able to identify and work with two kinds of anchor points – Smooth and Corner. You can identify each type by the way in which the associated direction points work.

Smooth Points

Select the point. Two direction points appear, connected to the anchor point by direction lines. Position your cursor on a direction point. Click and drag in a circular direction around the anchor point. The

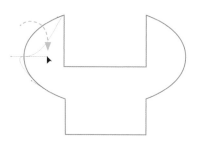

Smooth points guarantee a smooth, continuous transition of the curve segments through the point.

opposite direction point balances the move you make to the point, maintaining the precise alignment of both direction points in a straight line and guaranteeing the smooth transition of the curve through the anchor point.

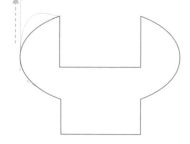

2 If you drag a direction point further away from or closer to the anchor point, the distance of the opposing direction point from the anchor point does not change.

Corner Points

Select the point. Two direction points appear, connected to the anchor point by direction lines. Position your cursor on a direction point. Click and drag in a circular direction around the anchor point. The opposite direction point does

Corner points are essential when you want to create a sharp change in direction at the anchor point:

not move. When you edit the direction points of a Corner point each direction point works completely independently of the other. This is what enables the sharp change in direction at the point.

Converting Points

Use the Convert Anchor Point tool to convert points from smooth to corner and vice versa. You can also use the Convert Anchor Point tool to retract direction points for smooth or corner points and also to convert a retracted anchor point to a smooth point.

Converting Smooth to Corner

1   To convert a smooth point to a corner point, use the Direct Selection tool to select a smooth point. Select the Convert Anchor Point tool.

2   Position your cursor on a direction point. Drag the direction point to convert the point to a corner point.

Converting Corner to Smooth

1   To convert a corner point to a smooth point, use the Direct Selection tool to select a corner point.

2   Select the Convert Anchor Point tool. Position the cursor on the selected anchor point. Drag off the anchor point to define the shape of the smooth curve.

3 Select the Direct Selection tool if you want to make further changes to the anchor point or its direction points. If you continue to use the Convert Anchor Point tool you may re-convert the point back to a corner point.

Retracting Direction Points

1 To retract direction points, select a smooth or corner point using the Direct Selection tool.

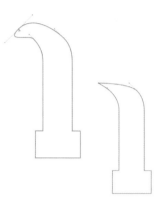

2 Select the Convert Anchor Point tool. Position your cursor on the anchor point. Click to retract the direction points. The incoming and outgoing curve segments redraw accordingly.

Creating a Smooth Point from a Retracted Point

1 To convert a retracted point into a smooth point, select the retracted point using the Direct Selection tool.

2 Select the Convert Anchor Point tool. Position your cursor on the retracted anchor point (one with no direction points). Drag off the point to create a smooth point.

Gradients and Gradient Meshes

A gradient fill is a gradual color transition from one color to another. You can also create multicolor gradients. A gradient mesh allows you to fill an object with multiple colors that blend into one another along smooth gradients.

Covers

Chapter Eleven

Applying a Gradient Fill

A gradient fill is a gradual color transition from one color to another. You can also create and apply multicolor gradients. Use the Gradient palette to create custom gradients and the Gradient tool to control the length and direction of the gradient.

You cannot apply a gradient fill to text until you have converted it to outlines.

The default Adobe Illustrator start-up file contains samples of gradient fills. Click the Show Gradients button in the Swatches palette to see available gradients only in the Swatches palette.

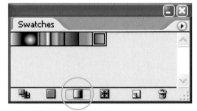

Hold down Shift as you drag the Gradient tool to constrain it to multiples of 45 degrees.

To apply a gradient, select an object using the Selection tool. Click the Fill box in the Toolbox to make it active. Then, click on an existing gradient fill in the Swatches palette.

2 Or, click the Gradient button, below the Fill/Stroke boxes in the Toolbox. This shows the Gradient palette and applies the current gradient to the selected object.

To apply a gradient fill to type, first select the text using the Selection tool, then choose Type>Create Outlines. Apply a gradient to the type outlines. Use the Gradient tool to create a gradient that flows through all the text characters:

STORM

Using the Gradient Tool

Make sure the gradient object remains selected. Select the Gradient tool. Position your cursor on the object. Click and drag. As you do so you will see a line. This line determines the direction and length of the gradient. For a linear gradient, the start and end colors fill any part of the object you do not drag the line over. For radial gradients, the end color fills the remaining area of the object.

Creating a Gradient Fill

Use the Gradient palette to create custom and multicolor gradients which you can then save in the Swatches palette.

1   To create a gradient, select an object using the Selection tool. Click the Fill box in the Toolbox.

If the Start and End color icons do not appear in the palette below the Gradient Ramp, click on the ramp. The color icons then appear.

2   Choose Window>Gradient, then Show Options from the Gradient palette menu (⊙). Choose Linear or Radial from the Type pop-up.

3   Click the Start color icon – the triangle on the top of the icon highlights. Mix a color using the Color palette. The color is applied to the gradient immediately. Or, you can drag an existing color swatch from the Swatches palette onto the Start color icon. Repeat the process for the End color icon.

4   Choose Radial or Linear from the Type pop-up. A Radial gradient uses the start color at the center of the gradient.

Hold down Alt/ option, then click on a color in the Swatches palette to apply a color to a selected Start/End color icon.

5   Specify an angle for a Linear gradient. Press Enter/Return to apply the change.

Angle: 47 °

6   You can drag the Start/End color icons to new positions on the Gradient Ramp to control the appearance of the gradient.

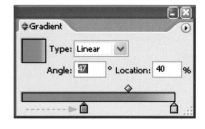

7   Drag the Mid-point slider to change the mid-point of the gradient – where both colors are at 50%.

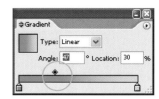

8   Alternatively, click on one of the Start/End or Midpoint icons, then enter a value in the location field to specify an exact location for the icon.

You can create gradients between different color modes, e.g. a process color to a spot color, but mixed-mode gradients are converted to CMYK process colors when printed or separated.

9   To save the gradient for future use, either drag the gradient fill box from the Gradient palette into the Swatches palette, or, as long as the gradient currently appears in the Fill box, click the New Swatch button in the Swatches palette.

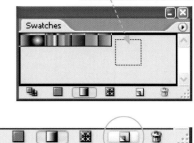

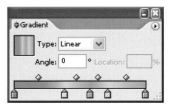

Creating a multicolor gradient

1   To create a multicolor gradient, click just below the Gradient Ramp to add color icons. Apply color to these additional color icons as you do for the Start/End icons. To delete a color icon from the gradient ramp, drag it out of the palette.

STORM

Creating a Gradient Mesh Object

To convert a gradient mesh object back into a standard path, select the mesh object, then choose Object>Path>Offset Path. Enter a zero in the Offset entry box then click OK to create a copy of the path behind the original gradient mesh object:

Offset Path

Offset: 0.15 in   OK

Joins: Miter   Cancel

Miter limit: 4

Keep mesh objects as simple as possible. Complex gradient mesh objects can slow performance, especially screen redraw. To maintain adequate performance it is better to create a number of mesh objects, rather than one large, complex mesh object.

Select an object, then choose Object>Create Gradient Mesh to start with a regular grid of mesh points.

You cannot create gradient mesh objects from compound paths, text or placed EPS files.

The Gradient Mesh tool provides a precise method for creating subtle color transitions within an object. In a mesh object you can have multiple colors flowing in different directions with smooth color transitions. You can easily and precisely adjust and manipulate multiple color shifts using the mesh which defines areas of color.

1 To create a Mesh object, select an object. Click on the Gradient Mesh tool.

2 Place your cursor in the object. The cursor changes to the Gradient Mesh cursor.

3 Click. A mesh point is added together with mesh lines which divide the original path into areas referred to as patches. The curvature of the mesh lines depends on the shape of the path of the original object.

4 To add further mesh points, select the Mesh tool, then, either click on a mesh line to create another mesh point on the line, or click elsewhere within the object to create a new series of mesh line divisions.

Adding Color to a Gradient Mesh

There is a variety of techniques for adding color to a gradient mesh. You can select a mesh point, then apply color using the Swatches or Color palette and you can drag and drop color swatches onto a mesh point or into a mesh patch.

Edit mesh points and mesh lines using either the Direct Selection tool or the Gradient Mesh tool to change how the mesh gradients flow across the object.

Adding color to a mesh point

1 To add color to a mesh point, select the Direct Selection or the Gradient Mesh tool.

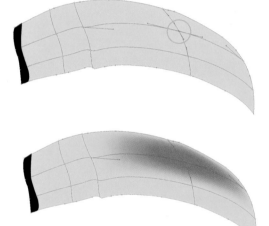

2 Click on a mesh point to select it. (Make sure that only one mesh point is selected.)

3 Click on a color swatch in the Swatches palette.

4 To drag and drop color onto a mesh point, select the mesh point using the Direct Selection tool. Drag and drop a color swatch onto the selected mesh point. Color is applied to the point and radiates out from the point.

Adding color to a mesh patch

1 Select the Direct
Selection tool, then
click on a mesh
patch to select it.
When you select
a patch with the
Direct Selection
tool, all mesh
anchor points on
the patch appear as
solid, blue squares.

2 Click on a color
swatch in the
Swatches palette to
add color to the selected mesh patch. The color fills the patch and
radiates out into neighboring patches. Alternatively, you can drag
color slider triangles in the Color palette to define a new color for
the selected patch.

3 To drag and drop color into a mesh
patch, select the mesh object using the
Selection or Direct Selection tool.
Drag and drop a
color swatch into one
of the mesh patches.
The new color fills
the mesh patch
and forms a color
transition into the
neighboring patches.

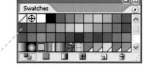

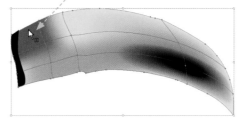

Editing a Gradient Mesh

It is best not to select a gradient mesh object with the Gradient Mesh tool as, in doing so, you can sometimes add new mesh lines.

Once you have created a mesh object you can edit mesh points to control the spread of color in the shape.

1 To edit a mesh point, select a single mesh point using the Direct Selection tool. Four direction lines appear at the mesh point (see page 155 for information on editing direction points and lines).

Editing mesh points and mesh lines follows the same basic principles as editing anchor points and direction lines. (See pages 153–155.) You can edit mesh points using the Gradient Mesh tool, but be careful not to inadvertently create additional mesh lines.

2 Select the Gradient Mesh tool for further editing of the mesh point, or continue to use the Direct Selection tool. Position your cursor on the selected mesh point, then click and drag to reposition the point. The mesh lines are reshaped accordingly.

3 Using the Gradient Mesh tool, hold down Shift, then click and drag the mesh point, to constrain the movement of the mesh point along the existing mesh lines.

4 Place the cursor on a direction point, then drag to edit the shape of the mesh lines. Or, hold down Shift then drag a direction point to rotate all direction lines uniformly at the same time.

You can also use the Direct Selection tool and Convert Anchor point tool to edit mesh points.

Deleting a Mesh Point

1 Select a mesh object using the Selection or Direct Selection tool. Select the Gradient Mesh tool. Hold down Alt/option, then click on the mesh point you want to delete.

Graphs

There are nine graph types to choose from in Adobe Illustrator. They are: Column, Stacked column, Bar, Stacked bar, Line, Area, Scatter, Pie and Radar graphs. This chapter uses the example of a simple Column graph to demonstrate the principles of creating and working with graphs in Adobe Illustrator.

Covers

Chapter Twelve

Creating a Column Graph

The initial procedure for creating graphs is the same for all graph types available in Illustrator. Once created, each graph type can be manipulated and customized using a variety of options dependent on the graph type. The following example shows you how to create a simple Column Graph.

1   To create a column graph, select the Column Graph tool. Position your cursor on the page then click. The Graph dialog appears.

Graph		
Width: 3 in		OK
Height: 3 in		Cancel

Enter Width/Height values for the graph then click OK.

2   Alternatively, select the Column Graph tool, position your cursor, then click and drag to define visually the size for your graph.

3   Enter data for the graph in the Graph Data palette. (See page 169 for information on entering and manipulating data in the Graph Data palette.)

	Europe	USA	Japan				
"2005"	10.00	13.00	14.50				
"2006"	17.00	24.00	27.00				

4   Click the Apply button to see the data plotted in the graph. Move the Graph Data palette if necessary to preview the graph in the Illustrator window. Click the Close button when you finish entering data.

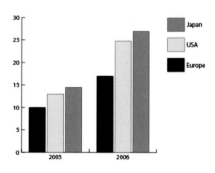

The Graph Data Palette

If you want to use numbers as category labels, as in this example, you must enclose the figures within quotation marks, otherwise Illustrator plots the figures as values in the graph, giving unintended results.

The Graph Data palette offers a spreadsheet-like environment for entering the numerical data and labels used to plot the graph.

1 To enter data, click in a cell to activate it. A thick black border indicates a selected cell.

2 Enter numeric data or text labels using the keyboard. Characters or numbers you type appear in the data

	Europe	USA	Japan	Korea	
"2005"	10.00	14.00	14.50		
"2006"	17.00	24.80	27.00		

entry line at the top of the window. Press the Tab key to accept the entry. The data is entered into the active cell and the highlight moves to the next cell to the right.

When you first create a new graph, the first cell in the Graph Data palette is highlighted and has a default value of 1. With the cell highlighted, press the Delete key to remove this value before you start to enter values into other cells in the palette.

3 To edit an existing entry, move to the cell so that it is selected, then use the data entry line to make changes as required. Press Enter/Return, Tab or an arrow key to accept the changes and move the highlight to another cell.

Controlling the width of cells

Press Enter/ Return to move the highlight to the next cell down. Press the arrow keys on your keyboard to move the highlight one cell up, down, left, right.

1 To make cells wider, so that long data entries are fully visible, click the Cell Style button. Enter a value for the column Width (up to 20 characters). This has no effect on the proportions of the graph – only how data is displayed in the Graph Data palette.

Cell Style		
Number of decimals: 2	digits	OK
Column width: 12	digits	Cancel

To create a pie chart, plot data in the Graph Data palette following the model below:

Europe	USA	Asia	Africa	
24000.00	62000.00	28000.00	14000.00	

2 Alternatively, position your cursor on a column dividing line. The cursor will change to a bidirectional arrow. Click and drag to change the width of the cell manually.

24.8	Europe
"2005"	10.00
"2006"	17.00

The Graph Type Dialog Box

For each graph type, there is a range of options in the Graph Type dialog box for customizing its appearance. You can also use the Graph Type dialog box to change the graph type used to plot the data entered in the Graph Data palette. For example, you might decide to change a Column Graph into a Line Graph.

The following instructions refer to a Column Graph. Each graph type has options specific to that type of graph.

Changing graph types

1. Use the Selection tool to select the graph, choose Object>Graph>Type. Click one of the graph type buttons to change the graph to another type.

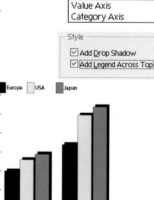

Changing graph options

1. Select a chart using the Selection tool. Choose Object>Graph>Type. Make sure the Options pop-up is set to Graph Options.

The type of data and the way you enter it in the Graph Data palette may mean that when you choose a different graph type you get unexpected or unintended results. For example, changing a Column graph into a Pie graph will not produce an acceptable result as the initial presentation of the data for each of these two graph types needs to be different.

2. Use Style options to add a standard drop shadow and/or to position the legend across the top of the graph.

3. Change the Column Width value to change the width of the columns in the graph. Change the Cluster Width value to specify the width taken up by each series of columns.

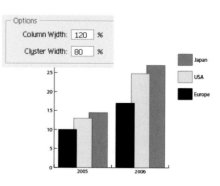

Changing Value Axis Options

1 Select a chart using the Selection tool. Choose Object>Graph>Type. Set the Options pop-up to Value Axis.

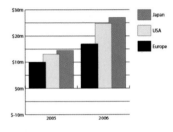

2 Select the Override Calculated Values option. Enter Minimum and Maximum values for the graph. By default, Illustrator calculates the minimum and maximum values from the data entered in the Graph Data palette. Enter a value for divisions to specify the increment used for the value axis.

3 Use the Length pop-up to set tick marks to the desired length and specify how many are drawn per increment along the Value axis. Enter Prefix and Suffix labels for the Value axis labels if necessary.

Changing Category Axis Options

1 Select a chart. Choose Object>Graph>Type. Set the Options pop-up to Category Axis. Use the Length pop-up to set tick marks to the desired length and specify how many are drawn per increment along the axis.

2 Select the "Draw tick marks between labels" option to place tick marks between each series of columns.

Editing Graph Data

After you create a graph you can edit the data and labels entered in the Graph Data palette, and you can change aspects of the graph such as the fill color of the columns or the stroke color and weight of lines, as well as the character attributes of text and value labels.

Illustrator creates graphs as a series of grouped objects. As long as the graph remains grouped you can return to the Graph Data palette to edit the data from which the graph is plotted. Any changes you make automatically update the graph when you click on the Apply button, or close the palette. However, you lose the dynamic link between data in the Graph Data palette and the graph if you ungroup the graph.

As a precaution, before you ungroup a graph to make further changes to its appearance, make a copy of it. In this way you can return to a version of the graph which still retains a live link to the graph data, in case you need to change the original data.

1 To edit graph data, select the graph using the Selection tool. Choose Object>Graph>Data to show the Graph Data palette.

Type...
Data...
Design...
Column...
Marker...

2 Make changes to the data and labels. Click the Apply button to preview changes in the Illustrator window.

Click the Revert button to return the data in the Graph Data palette to the stage it was at when you last clicked the Apply button:

3 Click the Close button to accept the changes. Click the Save button in the Warning dialog box if you closed the Graph

	Europe	USA	Japan
"2005"	10.00	22.00	14.50
"2006"	17.00	24.80	27.00

Data palette without first clicking on the Apply button.

Some graph options such as font size and column markers may revert to their defaults if you make changes to the graph data.

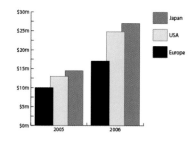

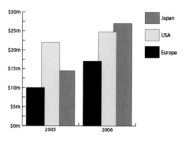

Changing Graph Attributes

As well as editing the graph data and using the standard options available in the Graph Type dialog box, you can change aspects of the graph such as the fill color of the columns or the stroke color and weight of lines, as well as the character attributes of text and value labels.

Illustrator creates a graph as a series of grouped objects. Use the Group Selection tool to select related aspects of the graph, e.g. all the category labels or all the columns in a series, before making changes to their position or appearance.

Changing colors in a graph

1 To change the color of columns, select the Group Selection tool.

2 Click once on the legend box of the series you want to change to select the legend box only. Click the same legend box again to select the columns which are grouped to that legend box.

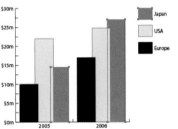

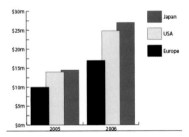

3 Make sure the Fill box is selected in the Toolbox. Click on a color swatch in the Swatches palette to change the color of the legend box and related columns.

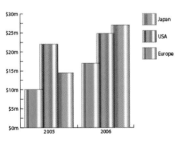

Changing the formatting of category labels

1 Select the Group Selection tool. Click twice on one of the category labels.

2 Use the Character palette to change the formatting of the labels.

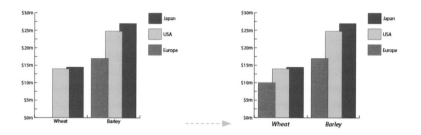

Customizing standard graph attributes

You can use the same Group Selection tool techniques to customize settings for graph attributes such as drop shadows and full width tick marks created using the Graph Type dialog box.

1 Select the Group Selection tool.

2 Click twice on one of the drop shadow boxes to select all the drop shadows, or click twice on a full width tick mark to select all the related tick marks.

3 Make changes to fill and stroke color and stroke weight settings as required.

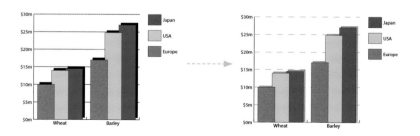

Filters and Effects

Adobe Illustrator ships with an extensive range of filters which you can use to change your artwork in various ways. The Illustrator filters alter, enhance or distort either the paths from which objects are created or their fills. The Photoshop filters work on rasterized (bitmap) objects and in RGB mode only.

As the primary function of Adobe Illustrator is to create vector based artwork, this chapter aims to give you a feel for some of the Illustrator filters and effects. Take time to experiment with the various filters and effects as they offer a great number of creative possibilities.

Use Effects to change the appearance of an object without changing the underlying shape of the object itself. You can use the Appearance palette to edit the settings you applied to create an effect.

Covers

Chapter Thirteen

Pucker and Bloat Filter

Pucker and Bloat, depending on the values you choose, can produce dramatic or subtle results – often the subtler results are more usable.

Photoshop filters, available in the Filter menu only, work in RGB color mode and on rasterized (bitmap) objects. Choose Object>Rasterize to convert an object into bitmap if required.

Pucker creates sharp, spiked shapes by curving paths inward from the anchor points and moving anchor points outward. Bloat creates the opposite effect – rounded, bloated shapes, by curving paths outward from the anchor point and moving anchor points inward.

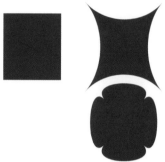

1 To Pucker or Bloat an object, select the object using the Selection tool.

2 Choose Filter>Distort>Pucker & Bloat.

You can apply Pucker & Bloat as either a filter or an effect. The advantage of using Pucker & Bloat from the Effect menu is that you can edit effect settings as many times as required to achieve the result you want. Using the filter changes the underlying objects which makes it much more difficult to change the results at a later stage.

3 Drag the slider toward Pucker or Bloat to create the effect. Or, enter a value in the % entry box from -200 to 200.

4 Select the Preview checkbox to see the results of the effect before you OK the dialog box.

Roughen Filter

The Roughen filter adds points to a path and moves them randomly inward and outward to roughen, or distort the original shape of the path.

1 To roughen an object, select an object using any of the selection tools. Choose Filter>Distort>Roughen.

Select the Preview checkbox to preview the result before you OK the Roughen dialog box.

2 Use the Size slider or enter a % value (0-100%) to specify how far from the original path anchor points can be moved.

3 Use the Detail per Inch slider or enter a value (0–100) to determine how many extra points can be added per inch along the path.

To edit settings, such as Roughen or Pucker and Bloat, applied as an effect, show the Appearance palette, then double-click the Roughen/Pucker & Bloat entry to return to the appropriate dialog box where you can edit the existing settings.

4 Select the Corner points option to create a sharp, jagged edge. Select the Smooth points option to create a smoother, softer edge effect.

Stylize Filters

Use Stylize filters to add a drop shadow to objects, to round corners and to add arrowheads to the ends of open paths.

1   To create a drop shadow, choose Drop Shadow from the Stylize sub-menu. Enter an "X" value to move the shadow horizontally away from the original object. Enter a "Y" value to move the shadow vertically away from the original. Enter a Darkness value to control the color of the shadow.

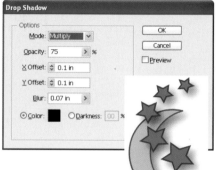

2   Choose Round Corners to create rounded corners on an object. Enter a Radius value to determine how rounded the corners become.

3   With an open path selected, choose Add Arrowheads. Click the Left/Right arrow buttons to choose from the available styles. Use the Start or End boxes to specify and preview the arrowheads. Use the Scale % entry box to specify the size.

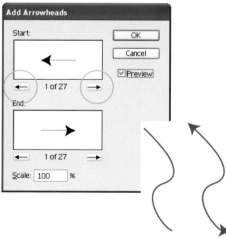

Effects

For an object with an effect applied, you can choose Object>Expand Appearance to create objects that are permanently changed – the equivalent of applying a filter. You can no longer edit the settings used to create the effect. To make further changes you must edit the individual shapes.

An Effect is one type of appearance attribute. When you apply an effect to an object, it changes the appearance of the object, not the original shape of the object itself. There is no limit to the number of effects you can apply to an object. The effects you apply to an object are listed in the Appearance palette (see pages 90–91). Use the Appearance palette to modify or delete effects.

1 To apply an effect to a selected object or group, choose Effect in the menu bar. Choose an effect from the list of effects.

2 Create settings, depending on the effect chosen, as required. The effect changes the appearance of the object. The object itself does not change.

Many of the Illustrator effects available in the Effects menu also exist as commands or functions elsewhere in Adobe Illustrator.

3 To edit the effect, make sure the Appearance palette is showing, then double-click the effect.

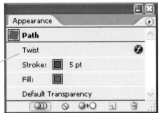

4 To apply an effect to a fill or stroke of a selected object, first click the Fill or Stroke entry in the Appearance palette, then apply the effect. For example, you can Scribble and Tweak (from the Distort sub-menu) the stroke of an object, without affecting the fill.

An effect allows you to change the appearance of an object whilst preserving its underlying shape.

To apply an effect to a layer you must target the layer first (see page 74).

5 To remove an effect from a selected object, click on the effect entry in the Appearance palette, then click the Wastebasket at the bottom of the palette. Or, drag the entry into it.

3D Rotation

When you rotate a 2D object you are limited to changing the X and Y axes. Using 3D effects introduces an additional axis – the Z axis, which lies perpendicular to the front surface of the object.

You have access to 3D rotation controls when you revolve or extrude an object and you can also rotate 2D objects in a 3D space using the 3D Rotate Options dialog box.

1 Select a 2D object to rotate, then choose Effects>3D>Rotate to access the 3D Rotate Options dialog box. Or, use the same set of controls that are available within the 3D Revolve and 3D Extrude & Bevel dialog boxes.

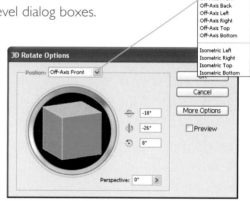

2 If you want to change the axis used for the rotation, use the Position pop-up menu to select a different option. Off-Axis Front is the default.

3 To specify rotation for the object's X, Y and Z axes, enter a value in the appropriate axis entry box.

4 Alternatively, to rotate the objects visually, position your cursor on each edge of the track cube. Notice the different edge colors as you do this. The colored edges correspond to the color of each rotation icon next to the numeric entry boxes. Drag a red edge to adjust the object's X axis rotation manually. Repeat

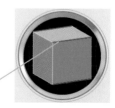

this process as required, dragging the green edge to manually adjust the object's Y axis and the blue edge to adjust the object's Z axis.

5 To rotate an object freely along all axes, position your cursor inside any of the track cube faces then drag. To constrain the rotation to the global axis, hold down Shift, then drag the X or Y axis edge of the track cube.

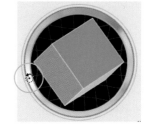

6 To rotate around the global Z axis, drag the blue circle surrounding the track cube in a circular direction.

You can also use the Perspective control in the 3D Extrude and Bevel and the 3D Revolve dialog boxes.

7 Enter a value in the Perspective entry box, or drag the Perspective pop-up slider to add perspective to the rotation effect.

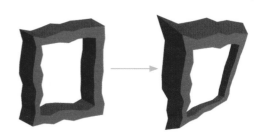

3D Extrude and Bevel

High Bevel Height settings can cause the extrude to self-intersect. This can sometimes cause unexpected results:

Reduce the setting or edit the shape as necessary to prevent this happening.

You can enter a value from 0 to 2000 in the Extrude Depth entry box.

The Extrude effect adds depth to an object by extending it along the Z axis. For example, you can extrude a circle to form a cylinder, or a rectangle to form a cube.

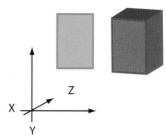

Extruding an object

1 Select an object, then choose Effects>3D>Extrude and Bevel.

2 Off-Axis Front is the default axis used to extrude an object. If you want to change the axis used to create the extrusion, use the Position pop-up menu to select a different option.

3 Use the Extrude Depth entry field, or drag the pop-up slider to control the depth of the extrusion.

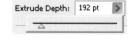

 50 pt

 100 pt

A bevelled edge appears along the depth or Z axis of the object.

4 Click the Extrude Cap On button () if you want the object to appear solid. Click the Extrude Cap Off button ( ) if you want the object to appear hollow .

Cap On   Cap Off

Applying a bevel to an object

See pages 185–186 for information on applying surface shading and controlling lighting effects for a 3D object.

1 To create a bevelled edge on an extruded shape, select an option from the Bevel pop-up menu.

2 Click the Bevel Extent In button ( ) to form the bevel from the original shape. Click the Bevel Extent Out button ( ) to add the bevel to the original shape. This makes the object appear larger.

After you apply a 3D effect, use the Appearance palette to modify or remove it. See pages 90–91 for information on using the Appearance palette.

Extent In   Extent Out

3 To control the extent of the bevel, enter a value from 1–100 in the Height entry box, or drag the Height pop-up slider.

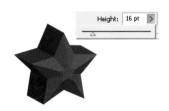

3D Revolve

3D Revolve creates a circular profile of an object around the global Y axis. The global Y axis is often referred to as the revolve axis. For best results with 3D Revolve start with an object that defines half the 3D object you want to create. The start object should also be vertical and front-facing. You can use closed or open paths with 3D Revolve.

1 To revolve an object in 3D, select a path. Choose Effect>3D>Revolve. To partially revolve the object, enter a value less than 360° in the Revolve Angle entry box. To revolve the object completely, leave the value set to 360°.

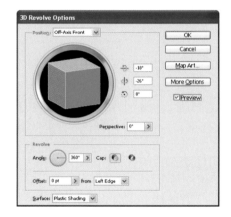

2 Click the Revolve Cap On button () to create an object with a solid appearance. Click the Revolve Cap Off button ( ) to make the object appear hollow.

3 If required, enter a value from 0–1000 in the Offset entry box, or drag the pop-up slider to specify a distance between the global Y (revolve) axis and the shape.

Original path   Offset = 0   Offset = 30
                        Left Edge   Left Edge

After you apply a 3D effect, use the Appearance palette to modify or remove it. See pages 90–91 for information on using the Appearance palette.

4 Choose Left Edge or Right Edge from the second Offset pop-up menu to set the axis around which the object revolves.

3D Lighting and Shading

Shading and Lighting options are available in the 3D Extrude and Bevel, Revolve and Rotation dialog boxes. For Plastic and Diffuse shading you can add lights, change the light intensity, and reposition the light source to manipulate and enhance the lighting effects for an object.

1 Use the Surface pop-up to choose a shading effect. Wire Frame and None do not have additional lighting options.

2 To display additional options to create custom lighting effects, click the More Options button (becomes Fewer Options). When you create a 3D effect, such as Extrude and Bevel or Revolve, Illustrator applies a single light to the object. The light square specifies the light source. Drag the light square to reposition the light source.

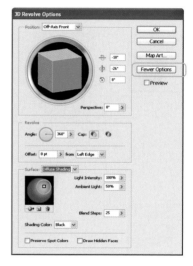

3 For a selected light square, click Move Light Back button ( ) to position the light behind the object. Click the Move Light Front button ( ) to move a selected light square in front of the object.

4 Click the New button ( ) to add a new light. New lights appear in the center of the light sphere. To delete a selected light source, click the Delete Light wastebasket button. Plastic and Diffuse shading effects must always have at least one light square.

...cont'd

5 Enter a value in the Light Intensity entry box, from 0%–100%, or drag the pop-up slider, to control the intensity of the directional light source. Enter a value from 0%–100% in the Ambient light entry box, or drag the pop-up slider, to control the overall lighting of the object. Adjusting the ambient light affects the brightness of all surfaces equally.

Highlight Intensity and Highlight Size controls are only available for the Plastic Shading option.

6 Enter a value from 0%-100% in the Highlight Intensity entry box, or drag the pop-up slider, to make the effect of light reflecting off the object more or less pronounced. Use higher values to create a more reflective shining surface. Use the Highlight Size control to increase or decrease the size of the highlight area on the object.

Hidden Faces are the shapes created at the back of a 3D object, and are typically not visible. Select Draw Hidden Faces if you intend to expand the 3D object then delete some or all of the frontmost shapes to reveal shapes behind.

7 Use the Blend Steps setting to control the smoothness of highlight to shade transitions across the surfaces of the object. Enter a value from 1–256, or drag the pop-up slider. Higher values produce smoother shades by using a greater number of paths to create the effect. You should bear in mind that smoother shades create more complex artwork which can take longer to print.

Preserve Spot Colors is only available if the shading color pop-up is set to Black.

8 Black is the default color used to create the shading for an object. To specify a different shading color, choose Custom from the Shading Color pop-up, then click the color box which appears. Use the Color Picker dialog box to select a shading color.

Index

S

T